Promise to my

Promise to my Mother

Margaret felt intense guilt for leaving her mother behind in Cyprus. She left for England after the 1974 invasion so her young family could live in safety. Margaret's mother, Nouritsa, survived the horrors of the 1915 Armenian Genocide that left her orphaned at a young age. Nouritsa had managed to escape to Cyprus and put her life back together, raising a family of her own. When Margaret left, Nouritsa had to face the heartache of being separated from her family once again. Though she tried, Margaret was unable to bring Nouritsa to England to be with her. Margaret knew, however, that Nouritsa desperately wanted someone to "tell the world" about what happened to her as a child. Nouritsa did not see any justice in her lifetime and so Margaret promised she would write her story so it will not be forgotten. This is the story about that promise.

Authored by Margaret Karakatounian and Haig Kiremidjian

© 2021

Contents

Prologue

In the 1940s, when I was a young girl, my mother would tell me stories as I went to bed. These stories, however, were not about princesses but instead about her traumatic childhood. She was one of the many Armenian children that lost their family in the most horrific manner during the 1915 Genocide in Ottoman Turkey. She would pause several times to compose herself as she told me these stories with deep emotion and tears in her eyes. We would then cry together until I fell asleep. Why would she torment her child with these horrific stories? At the time, I thought nothing of it. Thinking about it now, however, I can see this was not appropriate but I do not believe she meant me any harm. Her stories caused me to have many nightmares but they also brought me closer to my mother. In this way, she bonded with me but I also think she may have gone further with the stories than she had planned. She suffered so much as a child and this must have affected her psychologically. My mother was thrown in at the deep end of life. She had to toughen up fast in order to survive. She had very little education and only knew how to cook, clean and raise children. As such, she may have used this opportunity with me to vent her anger. I was captivated by what she told me and that probably encouraged her to continue. Additionally, in those days there was no television or radio so telling stories was a common way to pass the time. Many years later, I fought a successful battle against cancer. During this time, I was assigned a counsellor to help me through it all. I found myself telling the counsellor about my mother and the stories she would tell me as a child. In their assessment, my mother was undergoing therapy herself by telling me these stories and that she may have inadvertently caused me harm in the process.

The story to follow is in three parts. In part one I cover my life growing up in Cyprus and the political troubles I lived through as Cyprus gained its independence from Britain. It includes how my husband left France for Cyprus and his time working as a Cinema Projectionist for the British Army in Cyprus. It also covers our ordeal as a family living through the 1974 Turkish invasion of Cyprus. This invasion awakened the fear of Turks I had developed due to stories my parents told me about the 1915 Armenian Genocide they lived through. In part two, I describe the difficulties we faced as we decided to emigrate from Cyprus. These difficulties include my traumatic journey through Europe by train, my short time living in Paris and subsequent travel to England where we struggled to get a foothold. All along, I carried with me the guilt of leaving my parents. My mother in particular was upset but promised to forgive me if I "tell the world" about the Armenian Genocide she experienced as a child.

In part three, I tell my parents' horrific stories. I tell how many years later after leaving Cyprus, I filmed an interview with them as they both told their stories to the camera. My mother described her troubles around the time of the Genocide. She explained how, as a child, her family was murdered and how a kind Turkish family took her in and began raising her as a Muslim. She details how she was then collected from that family and returned to the Armenian Community. She also explains how, fearing for her life, she was forced to leave Turkey for Cyprus when Mustafa Kemal Ataturk rose to power. My father described how his family was forced to leave their home village of Soloz at the time of the Genocide. He explains how they struggled in their new life away from their home for a few years. He then details how they eventually went back to Soloz and lived under Greek rule for a time until Mustafa Kemal Ataturk rose to power and drove the Greeks out. He also explains how he followed the Greek retreat and ended up in Greece as a refugee for a time before finally arriving in Cyprus where he settled down. This all happened in the years 1914-1923.

With this writing, I am finally doing what my mother wanted by documenting what she went through. She wanted people to know what happened and to give a thought for people like herself who experienced such horrors as a child.

Part 1 - My Life in Cyprus
Growing Up

My father built the house where I was born. It was in Messolonghi Street, Agios Andreas, Nicosia. That house was such a special place for me with so many wonderful childhood memories. It was in a lovely tranquil location just outside the busy city. My mother gave birth to me at home with the help of a midwife on 24 November 1939. My mother's name is Nouritsa. My father's name is Hovhannes. I am the youngest of five children: Margaret, Arshalouys, Yeghisapet and Garabed (my only brother). I am Margaret, the youngest. I was named after my eldest sister who sadly died forty days after I was born. My mother would say we are her whole world. She had lost her family in 1915 but God had given us to her.

1945: Nouritsa, Yeghisapet, Arshalouys (back), Margaret (front), Garabed and Hovhannes.

We had a lot of space with the neighbouring houses far away from ours. I remember the extended family coming over on weekends and playing volleyball and football with my cousins. It was like a holiday retreat for them as they all lived inside the walled city of Nicosia without gardens or the outside space we had. We could make as much noise as we liked as our nearest neighbours were far away.

We would go for walks around the area and pick fresh mandarins and other seasonal fruits from the neighbourhood trees. In the evenings we would then have hours of fun singing together as a choir. We Kiremidjians had very good singing voices. Sometimes my father would play the violin and the oud for us to enjoy. Some nights, my mother would place a large kilim rug in the garden and we would sit there talking while staring up at the beautiful star-filled night sky. My childhood was a magical, happy time for me and completely free from fear. This was in stark contrast to my mother's childhood and I believe this is primarily thanks to the British rule in Cyprus.

Extended family 1925. Back row: Zareh, Chrissy, Krikor, Hovhannes. Middle row: Shenorig (Zareh's wife), Grandfather Toros, Grandmother Flora, Nouritsa. Front row: Mirijan (Zareh's oldest son), Harutyoun (Zareh's 2nd son), Michael (Chrissy's Son) and Flora (Chrissy's daughter).

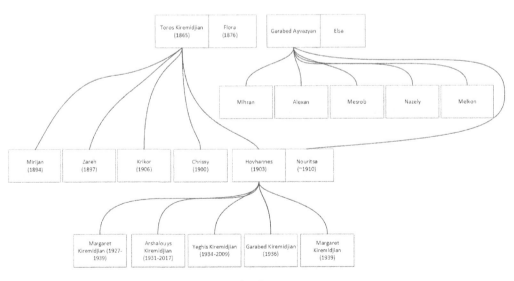

My family tree

As the youngest in the family, I think I was a little spoilt. My father would call me "dsaghighess", meaning "my flower". He said that when I was born I brought him good luck. My older brother Garbis would put me on the back of his bicycle and take me to school. I was very happy then. On my first day of Melikian Armenian Primary School, my mother took me. I did not cry as my brother, and sisters were there. I did not like school, however. This was mainly because of the teachers who were horrible to me. I did not realise it back then, but I believe I had some sort of learning difficulty. I have not been tested, but I think I suffered then and now from something like mild dyslexia. As much as I tried, I could not process information the same way the other children did. The teachers thought I was being rebellious and naughty. They would hit me on my hands with a ruler multiple times as if that would cure it. This put fear in me.

After completing Melikian Primary School, I went on to study at the Armenian Ouzounian Secondary School. Unfortunately, school life did not get any better for me. The teachers were similarly impatient with my inability to process information in the way they expected. They punished me regularly for not performing well in class. They also punished my sisters, through no fault of their own, for my failures. That is how it was.

As a teenager, I would cycle to school on a hand-me-down bicycle that used to belong to my older sister. At that time, the EOKA fighters were in full operation. EOKA was a Greek organisation that wanted Cyprus to become part of Greece. They wanted to get the British out and started a campaign of terrorism targeting the British soldiers and their families on the island. The school would often tell us to go home early because evening curfews would soon follow. On one such occasion, I had a terrible experience just before I reached home. I had cycled along the main road and stopped at the turning into my street. I was waiting for a break in the traffic so I could turn in safely. As I waited, a bus passed me by on my right. This bus was full of Greek commuters and, as they passed, I saw hands reach out from the windows and slap me. They knocked me over and I fell to the ground. I also heard them shout: "Stinking English!" at me. I cried and then made my way home. I could only imagine my blonde hair and green eyes made them think I was English and so targeted me as part of their EOKA movement against the English. Another time I was in my Girl Guide uniform cycling home when a taxi driver deliberately hit me from behind near a roundabout. I fell over with my bicycle and he then drove the car toward me to run me over. As the tyres neared my face, I thought that was the end of me. Just then, however, an English officer came to my rescue. He saw what happened and reacted speedily to stop the driver. He yelled: "Stop! You're going to kill the poor child!" After his intervention, the officer took me to the hospital and forced the driver and his passenger friend to come too. At the hospital, I spoke with the doctor in fluent

Greek. At that point, the taxi driver said to his friend in Greek: "Re, den einai Englaisa!" meaning, "Man, she is not English!" Again, I had been targeted for looking English. The officer helped me home. My bicycle was a complete write-off and my mother was so angry with me for being so late. She eventually realised what had happened and hugged and kissed me being thankful that I was unharmed.

As a child, I was a Brownie for a number of years and then a Girl Guide. Based at the Melikian Primary School, they would encourage us to look after vulnerable people and generally do useful things like cleaning up at campsites or retrieve the post for them from the post office. We also put on plays. I remember playing the lead role in Sleeping Beauty once.

Margaret as a Girl Guide (standing middle under flag).

I finished secondary school at age 14 and then went on to study shorthand typing at the Likion College. After that, I got my first job as a store assistant at Zako Limited, a Cypriot Haberdashery store. I did not like the job much as it required me to work long hours and to be on my feet all day. It did not pay much either so I left only after short time there. On learning of my search for a new job, my aunty Chrissy approached an English couple she knew that worked in the British Military. Aunty had two houses and this couple lived in one of those as her tenants. As my English was good, they found a role for me as a telephone operator but I had to be trained first.

The telephone exchange was located at Kykko Camp, an army camp near the Nicosia Airport. I travelled there by bus and was one of sixteen girls on a training programme that would last for three months. After this period they would select the best six so I worked extra hard to make the cut. In those days, pay was partly related to your age. I was one of the younger ones and so started at a "juvenile" rate, which was half the pay of the older trainee workers. The switchboard was a machine we had to operate to link incoming calls from military personnel to the destination recipients. I would sit in front of one of these machines alongside several other girls each with their own machine. We would all have headsets on and watch the flashing white and red lights that would light up in front of us when a request came through. On seeing a light, we would insert a cable into the audio socket next to it and say: "Hello, this is the Kykko Camp Operator, who would you like?" The voice on the line would state the person or office they wanted, for example: "General Smith". We would then know from memory that "General Smith" was on line 8 and so insert another cable into that socket. We would do this continually, as there was no shortage of incoming calls. The set up was that we would do this for 30 minutes and then take a break before returning to the switchboard. This regular time away from duty was necessary as it was so intense and would drive you mad otherwise.

While there, I made friends with many of the girls around. They, like me, passed the training successfully and continued on working there. I remember two Armenian girls: Jasmin and Anita, a Turk: Filize, a Greek: Sofia and a German: Helga. Jasmin confided in me that she had to fake her age on her passport to increase her age by 2 years to get the more senior role and so earn more money. We were actually the same age but officially, she was 2 years older. Filize was such a nice girl but when she got married to her Turkish husband, she had to quit her job. Her aunty, Julliende, also worked there and I got news from her that Filize's husband was very controlling and it was he that made her leave the job. Julliende later told me that Filize had died. She was only 19. I never got to know exactly how she died but suspect it was related to problems with her controlling husband. I was overcome with emotion and cried for her. I never thought I would ever cry for a Turk after the stories my mother had told me about what the Turks did to her, but my goodness I cried for Filize that day.

Margaret and Filize at Kykko Camp

Margaret at Kykko Camp

Margaret with sisters

While at Kykko camp, we had a few EOKA-instigated bomb scares. We were twenty girls and a few boys operating the lines. We also had three supervisors. The work was organised over three shifts: morning, afternoon and night. There was no public transport available for the workers to get to the camp. As such, the camp would organise its own transport. Due to the danger from the EOKA fighters, the transport would be a Land Rover with a special armed guard. One time, we were three girls in the Land Rover being taken to work. We were going to start the morning shift and so replacing the night shift. The Greek boys that worked there would normally do the night shift. Secretly, the EOKA fighters had placed a bomb under my seat. We got out of the car to start work as the Greek boys came off their shift made their way to it. As they were being driven home, the bomb exploded and injured them. Thankfully no one died. During these times I was really frightened. The thought of being blown up by one of these bombs was terrifying but the British reassured us by raising their security. They brought in sniffer dogs that could detect bombs and increased vigilance.

As I knew the head of Kykko Camp's Civilian Department, I was able to get my older sister, Arsha, a job there with me. We then would commute together in her car and so avoid being targeted by EOKA. After a few years working there, my cousin Flora also started work there. Flora was married to a British soldier, Gordon. As Flora's father had died when she was a baby, my father had been asked to give her away on their wedding day. I was very close to Flora. She was my aunty Chrissy's daughter

12

and lived next door to us. She was also part of our extended family group that would spend the days playing at our Messolonghi house "retreat" in my early days.

Left to right: Jenny, Margaret, Arshalouys, Ellie and Jasmin on duty at the switchboard.

On another occasion, a bomb was discovered behind the sand bags at the Telephone Exchange. The sand bags were placed everywhere to protect against any explosions. A soldier managed to neutralise and remove the bomb successfully. But it was another reminder of the risks we worked and lived under. It added to our worries as we would regularly be under curfews.

During this time I would be invited to the officers mess dinner dances but my father would not allow it. Occasionally he would allow me to go to afternoon tea dances at the Acropole Hotel but only if my brother and friend Janine would go. When we went, we would go in a big group of friends including my future husband Robert. My cousin Lucy and I knitted a pullover for my brother once. This was so he would take us in his car for a trip to the Troodos Mountains. It was cold up there but he did not have a suitably thick pullover. In Cyprus you would not need such a pullover even in the winter. The only time you did was if you went up to the mountains where the temperature would get much lower. Even after this, I had to push him to take us. I would attack him with my pillow and start a pillow fight with him until he gave in and agreed to my wish. Troodos was beautiful with snow-covered trees. We stayed at a lodge which had an open fire. We would go out in the snow and then come back and dry ourselves by the fire. We would drink whiskey there but instead of ice, we would put snow in it. We would drink a lot but knew our limits and would never get drunk.

In the late 1950s, Archbishop Makarios came back from his exile in the Seychelles. Makarios was a major religious and political figure at the time who initially wanted ENOSIS. "ENOSIS" is the term used by the Greeks meaning the unification of Cyprus with Greece. He was exiled by the British authorities as he was considered a danger. Makarios eventually changed his stance from ENOSIS to Cypriot independence and was allowed to return. In 1960, he became the first President of the newly independent Cyprus. As Cyprus got its independence, the British relocated their armed forces to the bases they held on to as part of the agreement. This meant our telephone exchange in Kykko Camp in Nicosia was relocated to Dhekelia on the outskirts of Larnaca. Independence meant no more British rule but they would continue to have two sovereign bases in Dhekelia and Akrotiri. Travelling to Dhekelia, however, meant a one and a half hour daily commute for me.

Working in the British Bases was very tiring due to the regimented nature of the organisation. While there, an opportunity came my way to work for the British Forces Broadcasting Service, the "BFBS". I thought working in a more civilian organisation like the BFBS would mean a relaxation of the regiment so I took it. It turned out to be just as regimented but, even so, I did not regret it. Working for the British Military, there were rules for everything. For example, when addressing an officer of the rank Major or Captain, we would have to call him "Sir" but when addressing a Corporal or Staff Sergeant we would have to call them by those exact titles and not by "Sir". We could never call them by their first names. When I moved across to the BFBS, my boss's title was "Station Controller" but because he had a rank equivalent Colonel, I had to address him as "Sir" too. This way of addressing people according to their rank was part of the culture, as was being punctual and always following orders without question if it came from a superior. A superior would tell you what to do and expect you to do it. There was no debating with them. If I ever disagreed with the instruction, I would have to say "Yes Sir" and obey anyway. If I felt strongly enough, I could complain but never at that point. I would have to follow the correct complaint procedures later.

I will describe more about my working life at the BFBS later as I was still working there in the run up to the 1974 conflict. For now, I want to tell you about my husband Robert and his background.

Robert

While at Melikian Primary School, I met a boy that would many years later become my husband. Robert arrived at our school from France. He was a few years older but was placed in a class with younger children as he did not speak Armenian. He was a nice looking young boy. One day while playing basketball, he accidentally pulled my shirt collar and it came off in his hand. The teacher, Miss Anahid, saw this and angrily instructed Robert to take my shirt and collar home to his mother who she decided was now responsible for repairing it. As Miss Anahid left us, I turned to Robert and said: "Don't worry about it. My mother will mend it. It's OK." I think that put me in his good books.

Robert was born in Nanterre, Paris on 23 May 1936. His parents, who were both Armenian Genocide survivors themselves, gave him a French and an Armenian name: Robert Manouk Karakatounian. Robert went to the Boulevard du Midi Primary School in Nanterre. Like many schools at the time, the grounds had a building for boys and a separate building for girls. His sisters went to the girls' school next door. The school was a fifteen-minute walk from their large five-story house. During the Second World War, his father Dickran would put an iron pot on his head and watch the German planes fly around from their attic room. He got a good view from there, being so high up and with a large dormer window.

One day while Robert and his siblings were at school, the sirens went off seven times meaning bombings were currently taking place. This had happened many times already and the children knew what to do. The elder students would take the younger students underground for safety. They would then wait for the single siren blast that would signal the danger was over. On this occasion, however, a bomb hit the school and killed some of the elder students in the explosion. The younger students were further away from the blast and so survived with only minor injuries. Robert's mother Ida ran to the school when she heard about it. When she got there, she saw police everywhere and feared the worst. As it turned out, her children were OK but the ordeal made her take action. Soon after, they sent their three eldest children: Jacques, Souren and Madeline to Chateau d'Auteuil, a boarding school outside Paris. They stayed there for about six months for their safety. This type of relocation program was one of many organised by the government in an effort to keep their citizens safe. The other siblings did not go, as they were too young and needed to be with their parents.

Robert remembers his grandmother Yester living with them at this time. She was a wonderful lady and Robert spent a lot of time with her. He learned to speak Turkish from her as she could not speak any other language. Robert at this time could only speak French and the Turkish he picked up from Yester. He would learn Armenian later in Cyprus. The Mayor of Nanterre eventually arranged for Robert's family to go to the village of Pressy for safety. Only Robert's father would need to stay in Paris as he had to continue to work. He would visit, however, at weekends. Pressy is located 400km from Paris and not too far from Lyon. They relocated to Pressy in 1943 and stayed there until the end of the war. Robert's father would visit once a month by train from Paris. He would bring money and stay a few days before returning. They stayed at a small bungalow but it had a large garden. There were many fruit trees in the garden and a well from where they would get fresh water. They also used the well as a fridge. Robert's mother would put meat in a container and lower it into the well to keep it cool. By doing this, the meat would stay fresh for up to a week.

Robert was happy at this time and spent a lot of time playing in the garden with his brother Souren. One day a local villager gave them an old unwanted deformed goat which had only one teat. It was very cute and they named her "Zezette". Robert and Souren put a rope around Zezette's neck and took her everywhere with them. She became their pet and they loved her. On their way to school Robert would load their school satchels on its back and she would carry the load for them. After school, they would call for Zezette and she would excitedly come running to them from the fields where she was grazing during the day. Robert's mother would milk Zezette and, from the goat milk, would make cheese and yoghurt. Robert and Souren would take Zezette with them when they went to collect mushrooms in the forest. They knew which mushrooms were safe to eat but their mother would still check them before cooking them when they returned home. Robert's mother had two un-hatched chicken eggs and, for some reason, she placed them with the un-hatched eggs of a duck she found in their garden. The mother duck lay on the chicken eggs as though they were her own. When they hatched, it was all very confusing as the baby ducks would go into the water but the baby chicks would not!

There was a farm not far from where they lived where they would buy butter. Robert says it was the best butter he has tasted even to this day. He would spread it on a slice of bread and sprinkle some sugar on it as a treat. He would also get excited when his father would bring him money on his visits and food that the Germans would give to him. The Germans, who had occupied Paris at this time in 1940, would bring Robert's father bread as payment for the work he would do for them making leather goods. Bread was very hard to come by during this period of severe rationing and so was very welcome. Ordinarily Ida would send Robert and the children out to get their ration of bread. During the war, they had to queue for this and were entitled to four baguettes per week. In Paris, Robert's father would make items from leather like satchels and brief cases. The Gestapo realised this during their occupation and wanted him to make things for them also. He had a deal with them: they would supply the leather and he would make the item they required out of it. Any leather leftovers would be his to keep. With the leftovers, he would make shoes for the family. Robert enjoyed his time in Pressy. Other than seeing a German plane crash in a field and catch fire, he did not see much of the war while there.

When the war ended, Robert had a very traumatic experience. His father had come to Pressy to help them prepare to return to Nanterre. He told Robert one day not to take Zezette with him to school. Robert wondered why but on his return, he found Zezette slaughtered and prepared for their meal! Robert and Souren cried and did not eat dinner that night. How can one eat one's friend? His father explained that they could not take Zezette with them back to Paris, but that was no consolation.

Robert's family in Pressy

Around that time, Robert's father got a telegram from Cyprus informing him that Ida's brother Hagop was to be married to a woman called Shenorig. Hagop wanted the family in France to go to Cyprus for his wedding. He had also sent some money to Dickran to help pay for the journey. Robert's family left their little house in Pressy after about a year and a half there. They loaded their luggage onto a horse and cart and went to the train station. On arrival in Paris, they barely had time to unpack when they began preparing for Cyprus. Then they got another telegram. This one was very upsetting. His own friend Sarkis had murdered Hagop! Sarkis had a sister who lived next to Hagop's shop and she was in love with Hagop. She did not like the idea of Hagop marrying someone else and so manipulated her brother to commit this crime. Hagop owned a photo studio where he would develop photographic film. While working there one evening, he had left the door to the shop open. His friend Sarkis walked in in a drunken state with a knife in his hand shouting: "I am going to kill you!"

Hagop replied: "You are drunk my friend" and grabbed the knife from him, throwing it away. Hagop then turned his back on Sarkis to continue his work. Sarkis retrieved the knife and, while laughing, stabbed Hagop in the back. Hagop made it to hospital and survived a few days but eventually died.

On hearing the news about her brother, Robert's mother was devastated and cried all night. She decided to go to Cyprus for the funeral and to help sort out Hagop's estate in place of what would have been the wedding. Robert's parents decided to leave Robert and Souren with their grandmother Yester and uncle Samuel as they were too young for the journey and work ahead of them. Robert was very upset at first but he was young and soon got used to it. His uncle looked after him very well. The rest of the family left for Cyprus. It took them 21 days to get there. They went to Marseille by train and then by ship to Beirut. From there they took another ship to Cyprus. When they got to Cyprus, it took a long time to sort out Hagop's estate. The legal process was long and took almost 2 years. In that time, the family decided to make a new home in Cyprus and leave France for good. Robert's father who was a leather goods maker opened a leather goods shop opposite the film developing shop. He made and sold leather items such as shoes, slippers and even gun holsters that were in demand among the Turkish community that lived there. He would also help run the film developing shop across from him when needed. Robert's brother, Jacque, had trained up as a film developer to take over the running of his uncle Hagop's old business. This was a new and thriving business at that time when people would take pictures on their cameras and have them developed in a special lab. These days you can do all this using a digital camera and printer.

After a year, Robert's father went back to France to visit Robert and Souren and to give his brother some money to continue to support his two sons while he was away. After another year, Robert's father was in a position to have his two sons come live with them in Cyprus. Therefore, he went back to France again and this time collected Robert and Souren and brought them back with him to Cyprus. Robert was 13 years old when he moved to Cyprus. His parents sent him to the Terra Santa Catholic School where they taught classes in French. This was ideal as Robert could not speak Greek or Armenian. On one occasion, the teacher was upset with Robert and hit him on his back very hard. When Robert's father saw his bleeding wound, he confronted the head teacher. He did not send Robert back to that school. Instead, he found an Armenian language tutor for Robert. After he learned some basics, he enrolled Robert into the Melikian Armenian Primary School where I met him for the first time.

Left to right: Souren, Yester, Uncle Samuel and Robert taken in 1947

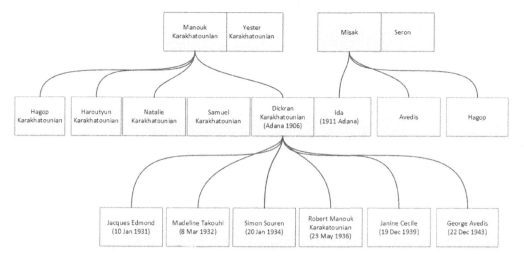

Roberts's family tree

Dickran, Robert's father in 1926

Pictures of Robert 1947 and 1974

Picture of Margaret and Robert at the Melikian Primary School in 1952

Years later, Robert left school and in 1952 got a job working in a textile shop for Mr Tateos Bodikyan in Nicosia. One day he was stunned when he saw Sarkis walk into the shop, the man that murdered his uncle Hagop several years back. Sarkis had been apprehended and spent time in prison but was now out. It is a good thing that Robert's boss, Mr Bodikyan was there at this moment. He saw the rage swelling up inside Robert as he stared at his uncle's murderer. It was obvious that Robert was about to pick a fight with him so he immediately called Robert to him and gave him an errand. Robert had to do what his boss said and so the situation was diffused.

At age 17, Robert started his working life at the AKC (Army Kinema Corporation). It was 1953 and he left home in Nicosia to relocate to Dhekelia, on the outskirts of Larnaca. The AKC managed many cinemas around the world to provide entertainment for the British Forces. The Armenians would call it the "Armenian" Kinema Corporation due to the large number of Armenians employed to work there. The British preferred hiring local Armenians ahead of the local Greek or Turks as, in their minds, Armenians were less of a threat during the EOKA movement against the British. This was a very real threat where EOKA would set off bombs as part of a campaign demanding the British give up rule in Cyprus. Robert quickly developed a good knowledge of the projectors and began to maintain and service them as well as projecting the movies for the audience. Maintaining and servicing them was not his responsibility but he did not want the technicians to touch them as he thought they may cause damage. The AKC recognised Robert's expertise as a projectionist and frequently got him to train others and set up new cinemas all over Cyprus. As a result he relocated a number of times over the following several years. Dhekelia, Cyprus became the AKC's headquarters after the British left Egypt following the Suez crisis. The AKC built a new building there for this purpose. The British shipped a lot of equipment from Egypt to the Famagusta Port. From there, they transported the equipment by road throughout their sites including to Episkopi, Limassol. They transported the equipment along the slow narrow roads that were there before the motorways were built. The transported equipment included Kalee 12, 18 and 21 projectors, films in reels, cabinets, tables, chairs etc. The old movie projectors required a lot of skill to run. In those days, a carbon arc would generate the projector light. As a result, it was much hotter than bulbs used later. Due to the intense heat, the film would have to continuously turn otherwise it would burn. The film was wrapped around a large reel and it was common for a single movie to be stored on multiple reels. This meant switching reels part way through the movie was necessary. To avoid disrupting the movie, it was common to have two projectors and so avoid having to stop to switch reels. At this time, the AKC also started to rent out television sets to the British soldiers. Robert managed to get one for his father who was so excited to be one of the first people to own a television set.

Robert was the second projectionist for the AKC and trained at the Apollon Cinema in Nicosia. When he started his job in Dhekelia, he earned £4.50 per week which in 1953 was very good pay. Robert's biggest problem in the early days working at the AKC in Dhekelia was the lack of access to food. As a non-British soldier, he was not allowed to use the army facilities but there was nowhere else that served food. There was a small sandwich shop opposite the cinema but that would be open for only a short duration. Robert remembers he would regularly go hungry – not for lack of money but for lack of availability. Eventually, after making some enquiries, Robert was allowed to use the cookhouse where soldiers got their food. Robert was at the Dhekelia AKC for one year before they moved him onto another AKC cinema in Karalaos Famagusta. This is where the movie Exodus, starring Paul Newman, was filmed. Robert remembers seeing Paul Newman while he was filming there. After a year at Karalaos Famagusta, they moved him onto the cinema in Episkopi Limassol. This was the first stereophonic cinema in Cyprus. Engineers came from England to set up the equipment with Robert's assistance. The first movie that played with stereophonic sound in Cyprus was Daddy Long Legs, a 1955 comedy musical starring Fred Astaire. After two years, they moved him on again, this time to Kermia in Nicosia. The cinema there was in a tent, the sort you have when a travelling circus arrives. During the winter, it would get very cold in that cinema. While based there, they gave Robert a caravan as an office room. As he was back in Nicosia, Robert moved back in with his parents. Their house was on Victoria Street in central Nicosia where the Armenian Church was also located. He bought a small Vespa scooter for £120 for the eight-mile commute. He stayed in Nicosia for the next five years. Robert did not mind moving around so much as he was single with no dependents. He did like being back with his parents in Nicosia as he missed them, however. As Robert now had access to the NAAFI army stores, he would buy Gin for his mother. She liked Gin.

Pictures of Robert working at the AKC

During his time back in Nicosia I saw Robert a lot. Then they relocated Robert to Dhekelia and we did not see each other again for a long while. The AKC was about to open a new cinema there called the Key Cinema. The first movie Robert presented there was "Carry on Nurse". It so happened that one of the star actors of the film was there at its showing. Robert remembers before starting the film, they ran tests to make sure all was ok. As they did so, however, the film tape snapped and the reel started spewing out tape all over the floor rather than have it automatically wrap around the second reel. The engineer yelled: "Stop the whole thing!" to prevent any permanent damage to the tape. Robert, however, shouted even louder: "No!" and speedily managed to collect the loose tape and wind it round the second reel. On seeing this, the engineer exclaimed "Wow! I have never seen anything like this." Robert later found the snapped part of the tape and glued them together to ensure the same would not happen at the next showing. To be a projectionist you had to have a deep understanding of the components of the projector and be prepared to act quickly to avoid serious problems.

On one occasion in the early 1960s, a bomb went off in the Dhekelia British Base. EOKA had planted the bomb in the canteen fridge. At the Base, there were two cinema screens. Robert was projecting the movie "Rock Around the Clock" on the main screen while his friend and colleague Girayr Sultanian was projecting on the second screen located in the canteen. At around 8pm the bomb went off in the second cinema. A few people were wounded but no one was killed. Luckily, the bomb was detonated while inside a fridge at the far end of the canteen. The military police rushed to the scene. They ordered Robert to stop the movie and turn on the auditorium lights as they searched for the terrorist. They did not find the EOKA perpetrator. Robert and the team were extra vigilant after that and regularly checked for anything suspicious in the cinema. EOKA was responsible for many terror attacks including blowing up buildings after they had been newly built. It is important to note that they were targeting the British Military and not the civilians. One time, Robert knew of a warning EOKA had given to his friend, Hagop Gazarian, working at the Stockwell Cinema in Episkopi. Hagop was responsible for transporting the cinema takings to the local Limassol bank for deposit. He had asked for an escort from the British but EOKA warned him that if he travelled with the British escorts he could be caught up in an attack. This information would come via word of mouth, as that is how EOKA operated. The EOKA operations made Robert uneasy but he did not think too deeply about them and just got on with life. EOKA, however, played a bigger and bigger part in our lives.

Married Life

I now turn to my early married life and what life was like for us in the late 60s and early 70s living in Cyprus. Robert had left school at 14 to start his working life. He did various odd jobs before starting work at the AKC aged 17. I knew him at school but did not see him again until his work brought him back to Kermia Nicosia several years later. During the time Robert was away, I became close friends with his sister Janine. Janine and I would go out together and sometimes do fashion shows at the Ledra Palace hotel. We would wear and model Vanity Fair dresses for the audiences. When Robert returned, he became part of my social group and we would regularly go out together as a group. Sometimes we would go to the freezing cold cinema where he worked with our blankets. It was very exciting, as we would see the latest movies before anyone else. At the AKC, they would show the very latest movies that were not available at the normal Cypriot cinemas. Robert was able to get us in as his special guests. This made us feel extra special, as ordinary Cypriots were not allowed in. At that time, very few people had a car but my brother was one of those few. He would let me drive his Fiat Millecento 1100 and I think I was one of the first females to drive in Cyprus. Robert would always make the sign of the cross when getting in as a passenger but I know he was joking. Later I taught him how to drive.

Pictures of Margaret driving a Fiat Millicento

In those days, it was not acceptable for women to drive or to ride a bicycle for that matter. Anyone doing so was considered a "tomboy", which was frowned upon at that time. I had already been cycling for a long while, however, through necessity as there was no other easy way to get about. Even so, the older people looked down at me for this but I took no notice. I belonged to the new generation who was about to change the perceptions of people in Cyprus. Now I had the opportunity, with my brother teaching me, to learn to drive. I was really pushing the boundaries and was proud of myself for doing so.

Pictures of social group in the mid-60s

After a few of years of meeting up like this, they relocated Robert to Dhekelia and we did not see each other for a long while. Then, Robert's parent began to urge him to get married and suggested me to him. My father approved and we got married in 1963. The ceremony was held in the Soorp Asdvadsadsin Armenian Church in Nicosia. Over a hundred people came to the service. Most of them came as they lived in the Armenian quarter of Nicosia very close to the church. After the church ceremony, we stood outside for a while handing out sweets and shaking hands with our friends and relatives. We then went to Robert's family house for dinner with my parents. After that, we went to our new home in Larnaca. We had rented a beautiful house there.

Pictures of wedding in 1963

We relocated a few times while in Larnaca and eventually had a new house built for us. This happened under very fortunate circumstances. There was a downturn in the economy and a local house builder was under pressure to let his workers go as there were no contracts coming in for him. He offered to build a house for us at very low cost so he could hold on to his workers until the economy picked up. We happened to be at the right place at the right time and got our house built for a fraction of the normal price.

Around this time, I started my new receptionist job at the BFBS that I consider the best I have ever had. But society at the time was very difficult for a young woman. If you did not stay at home and out of sight, you would attract the attention of unsavoury characters. After I got married to Robert, I frequently found myself travelling alone and being alone in the evenings through necessity. I knew of others in a similar situation that were violently harassed and feared something similar could happen to me at some point. In those days, it was not acceptable for respectable women to go out with a man on a date. As such, many men would go to cabarets to find loose women and if you happened to be out – they would assume you to be in that category and prey on you. This is also why many women did not want to divorce their husbands as by doing so you would fall into that category.

When I moved in with Robert, our work schedules conflicted such that we could not see each other that much. Robert was off most of the day while I worked, and he worked until midnight while I was off in the evenings. Only on holidays could we spend any time together. We did not have any other option as money was very tight and we both had to work. It did put a strain on our marriage but we got on with things. At 4pm on 3rd August 1967, I gave birth to my son Baret at the Central

Nicosia Hospital. The pregnancy for me was relatively easy and problem-free. I was working and active right up to labour. Afterwards, I stayed with my parents in Nicosia for a month. During this time, my parents took good care of me and even took me for a trip to the mountain village of Kakopetria to escape the Nicosia heat. Soon after, I moved back to Larnaca to go back to work. As Robert and I had to work, we arranged for my mother to look after Baret during the week. They lived in Nicosia and we lived an hour drive away in Larnaca. We would then visit at the weekend and see Baret and my parents. My mother was effectively raising Baret. I felt so bad about that but did not have any better options. Because of Baret spending his early years with my parents, we visited my parents a lot and spent time together. We also spent a fair amount of time with my sisters and brother and their families. Over the years our weekends were spent together either in Larnaca (where I and my sister Yeghisapet lived), Limassol (where by brother lived) or Nicosia (where my parents and my eldest sister Arshalouys lived). We had a lovely family life in the sunshine and seaside with each other. We loved each other and were very close. It was not until 1970 that we had Baret live with us. Although we dearly wanted that anyway, it was forced on us as my mother developed Bell's Palsy and was no longer able to take care of him. Bell's Palsy is a condition causing loss of control of facial muscles. We just about managed with Baret and our work schedules. While I was at work during the day, Robert would take Baret to his nursery and then go to work. I would take over looking after Baret in the afternoon, while Robert headed off to work. Our routine was like clockwork, anything that forced us to deviate from this would cause us big problems. This way, one of us was always with him.

At a young age, Baret developed croup and had us very worried. He needed his tonsils taken out and so underwent surgery. When he came out of hospital, he was coughing continuously which had us worried even more as this could affect the stitches in his throat. The doctors said there was nothing further they could do and that we just had to wait and see how he would recover. Robert and I got on our knees that night and prayed until morning. We gave him drops of warm tea to soothe his throat and reduce his coughing. I promised God that if Baret got better, I would take him to Jerusalem to see the holy land. Thankfully, Baret did get better and later I kept my promise. I took Baret to see the land where Jesus walked. My parents came with me but Robert could not as he had to work. We visited the Church of the Holy Sepulchre, the site where Jesus is said to have been crucified. We saw the stone where Jesus' body is said to have been laid after he was brought down from the cross. It was an amazing place but at the same time, we felt they were exploiting it for monetary gain. Baret also sensed the exploitation but enjoyed the experience.

We enrolled Baret at the Lion House Kindergarten English nursery where he went between 1970 and 1974. Around that time Jenny Agutter, the actress, also went to that school. I know this because her father, Derek, worked with me at the BFBS. He was the head of the BFBS in Cyprus – the official provider of entertainment to the British Armed Forces. Derek Agutter used to bring many famous people to Cyprus. I remember he managed to get Major Donald Craig, who was played by Rock Hudson in the blockbuster movie "Tobruk", to come to our base for the opening of the movie. He was a hero from the Second World War and came by helicopter to the BFBS offices where I met him. He was very tall and handsome and I got to know him a little as I had to greet him and show him around. The following day, he came again. This time it was unexpected. On this occasion, he brought me a red rose. I went red with embarrassment. I knew my boss was not in his office so I told him: "We weren't expecting you General, I don't know where my boss is but I'll call him on the tannoy system for you".

He said "No rush, I am enjoying your hospitality."

I had just brought him a glass of water when my boss finally came to reception. I was so relieved. "So sorry" said my boss "we didn't know you were coming."

"No problem" said the General "your receptionist took very good care of me." I went red again as I noticed my boss looking at the red rose in my hand.

At the BFBS, we had a number of socials and events organised. One time we hired three boats and sailed to Fig Tree Bay. We spent a wonderful day at the beach and swam in the sea. They arranged for a meze lunch with plenty of Saint Panteleimon wine and Keo beer. We listened to the popular Greek music of the day like Delphini Delphinaki by Marios Loizos and Ta Bedia Tou Pirea by Melina Mercury. As we sang these songs, Keith Rawlings the show producer who was on the boat with us, had an idea about a new show. He discussed the idea with me to do a program where I would translate popular Greek songs on air so that the British listeners could understand them. I would regularly talk with Keith including about my family's history escaping Genocide from Ottoman Turkey. I had told him about my parents' terrible childhood experiences and he encouraged me to capture their story on film. He said I should interview both my parents and even gave me a set of questions I should ask them to tease out the main elements of their past. I remember him saying to me about the possibility of bringing their memories to film: "Now that would make one amazing story!" As we returned to Dhekelia, there was a full moon as we sang and enjoyed ourselves. It was beautiful. We sang Greek and English songs but then they all wanted us Armenians to sing some Armenian songs. There were about 20 of us on two boats. It was mostly BFBS colleagues, many of whom were Armenian. Along with two of my Armenian colleagues, we sang: "Navagin

Mech" which is Armenian for "In the boat" and "Sev mazerov siroun aghchik" which is Armenian for "The lovely girl with the black hair". They all enjoyed our singing. I had learned these songs from my sister, Arshalouys. She and I would regularly sing these songs together as children. We had many other events, including many where special guest visitors would arrive. These included the boxer Joe Bugner, the actor/singer Harry Secombe among many others. Derek Agutter would organise these events. He would arrange for all the latest records from the music library to be played and we would dance until the early hours. In those days, music was stored on physical records and was not digitized. Thousands of these records were kept in a huge room from where they would need to be fetched when required. The BFBS lounge where we would host these events had patio doors that opened out onto a large patio. On one side of it, we had a beautiful pond that would be decorated with colourful lights. We had many lovely parties and socials at this time. The BFBS arranged a game of football between the British and the Armenians on one occasion. Robert played on the Armenian team, as did my young nephew Movses. I don't know much about football, but I know that after the game they would be hungry and thirsty. As such, I made sure I arranged a feast at the BFBS canteen for afterwards.

Robert and I would also attend many dinner dances around this time. On one occasion Adiss Harmandian, the singer famous in Armenian circles, was singing at one of them. He was very handsome and known as the "Armenian Tom Jones". I had one of his records and made sure he signed it for me.

This was our life for a time and I was joyful as Baret grew up in our home on the sunny island of Cyprus. Robert and I were both working and able to provide for him. I could not imagine at this point how events in the following years would completely change our lives.

1974 Invasion

Ever since I could remember, there were troubles in Cyprus. The British had taken over control of the island from the Ottomans in the early 1900s. At that time, the population was mainly ethnically Greek but there was also a significant ethnically Turkish population. The Greek population wanted Cyprus to become part of Greece. A major movement took hold, which they called ENOSIS or "Union with Greece". This movement resulted in numerous terrorist attacks over the years against the ruling British by a group called EOKA. I can remember many such cases, which resulted in the British regularly imposing curfews, and I had to stay at home. The British resisted EOKA and the ENOSIS movement but eventually realised they could not. Instead of giving in, however, they achieved an alternative outcome of Cypriot independence. This happened formally in 1960. The Cypriot Greeks were divided with some still wanting ENOSIS while the others accepted independence with a constitution set up to ensure rights for the ethnic Turks. This division between the

Greeks lead to civil war in 1974, followed by a Turkish invasion of the island. The civil war broke out on 15 July 1974 when the EOKA fighters supported by the Junta Government of Greece overthrew the Makarios Government. Over the next few days there was turmoil. In Larnaca, they rounded up the local Turkish Cypriots and held them captive in a local Greek school. This was to stop them from fighting. I remember driving past that school and seeing them looking out. They would make lewd comments and hand gestures as people passed them. I am sure similar events took place all over Cyprus.

Just prior to 15 July 1974 coup d'etat, Robert and I had planned a holiday to Beirut. I remember the day very well. We had packed our bags and closed up the house. We were getting ready to go to the airport. Robert was having his trousers altered at the "Jet" men's clothing store near Finikoudes, the Larnaca waterfront. He went to get them but found himself caught up in gunfire. As he returned to his parked car, shooting broke out. The EOKA fighters were attacking the police station near Robert's car. Robert speedily got into his car and drove off. He calculated that there would be a curfew imposed very soon so he collected me and we went together to the supermarket to get some supplies. The store was a Sinerghadigon, a Cypriot cooperative chain. When we got there, the shop owner was panicking and closing the shutters of the shop. Robert was a good regular customer and so managed to convince the owner to let him get some supplies before closing up. As Robert was grabbing a few items off the shelves, the man got a call and yelled out "They have killed Makarios! They will come for me very soon. Hurry up Robert!" This was because the man was a staunch public Makarios supporter. Robert and I then came home. The curfew started and lasted several days. During this time, the civil war was in full flow with bombings in Nicosia including the Melkonian Armenian School. As a result, my sister Arshalouys and her family (who lived in Nicosia) took my parents (who also lived in Nicosia) to the relative safety of the Troodos Mountains. Many of their Greek Cypriot neighbours had done the same, going to stay with their relatives that lived up there. My parents had no relatives up there and so had to hire a place in one of the villages.

On the news, we would hear of Greek Cypriots killing other Greek Cypriots. I would think to myself that if the Greeks would kill their own people they would not hesitate to kill Armenians. My young son, Baret, was very frightened at this time. He would hear all the talk of war on the news and between Robert and me. I would regularly discuss the situation with Robert. I recall pointing out how we were so isolated where we lived. Our house was in the middle of nowhere. What could we do if attacked? We were sitting ducks. We decided to make sure we switched off the lights at night so as not to be visible as far as possible. We frantically phoned both the British and French embassies for advice on how to stay safe. We also were in touch with Robert's friend and colleague Harry who worked at the Dhekelia base. He said that many people were moving into the various camps set up by the British in the two sovereign bases. We stayed in touch for a few days via phone as we stayed at home. There was gunfire in the fields near our house. Neither of us went to work for a few days as we tried to come up with a plan of what to do. We were not allowed out as curfews were imposed. It was even more frightening as we did not even know which soldiers were friends and which were enemies. If you supported Makarios you would be the enemy of one group and if you were against him you would be the enemy of the other. During this time, we could hear soldiers marching from the back of our house and hear tanks roaring. Robert got a call from work saying he had to come into work at the base. A curfew pass was organised for him.

Not long later, Turkey invaded Cyprus on 20 July 1974. They, along with Greece and Britain, were guarantors of the constitution. They claimed they had the right to do so due to the ENOSIS fighters trying to overthrow the Cypriot Government. They had an interest in Cyprus due to the population of ethnic Turks that made up approximately 20% of the total population. Robert was still going to work when this happened, which meant I would be home alone with my 6 year old son. All night we would hear tanks roaring and gunfire. Some of our neighbours had left for the mountains to stay in the relative safety with their families. My health deteriorated from the stress and I was unwell a lot. It was the same with Baret, he developed a stomach-ache. We were in fear for our lives. Turkey started the invasion from the north very early in the day. Although we lived on the other end of the island in the south, we could hear bombs and gunfire. This was coming from the Makenzie area near the beach in Larnaca. There was a large Turkish Cypriot minority population there. They were now fighting against both groups of Greeks from their enclave. They were fighting from the fear of what would happen to them. The British were helping the Turkish Cypriots to fight.

We were one of the few people left in Larnaca but we could not leave. During the day, we would see stray bullets hit the dry grass in the fields and cause fires. The news from the TV and radio instructed civilians like us to stay in centre of the house. We saw a man at the back of our house and asked what we can do to stay safe and how we can get some food. I was alone with Baret while Robert was at work. He told us there were Makarios' Greek Cypriot soldiers nearby distributing bread for the people to eat. He managed to get some for us. He invited us to his house and we went to stay there during the day. We felt a little safer at that time but we did not want to stay the evening so we returned home. Robert was back at that time too.

When Robert returned from work that day, I could see he was unwell. The smell from the mortars and the intense heat of the summer had made him sick. I got him to put his head in the fridge thinking this would help to cool him down and it seemed to work. Robert explained that earlier he had encountered some EOKA Soldiers and they were pressuring him to take up arms and fight the Turks. They were tormenting him but he managed to get away from them and get home. We heard on the radio that Makarios was still alive. He had set up a government base in Paphos and was now fighting back. This news gave us hope that peace may eventually be restored. Robert, still fuming at the way the EOKA fighters had treated him, prepared some Molotov Cocktails in case anyone attacked our home. He had learned from friends that by getting a bottle and filling it with something flammable like petrol and having a piece of cloth covering the top would make for an effective bomb. "If anyone comes to our house I will light the cloth and throw the bottle at them. We can fight back this way." In the midst of all this, Baret said to me: "Mummy, if the Turks come to our house we can hide in a place I found." He showed me to the bathroom. We had a cupboard there and inside was the laundry basket. He got in and covered himself with the clothes. He then closed the cupboard. "Excellent Baret. If they come you will hide there."

We eventually decided we would pick up my parents from Nicosia and make our way to the British Base in Dhekelia. My parents had gone to the mountains on 15 July but had come back. Staying in the mountains would have been a struggle for them as they would have to secure a place and did not know for how long. The bombings continued and took out many of the telephone lines making communication hard. Robert and I rushed to Nicosia to pick up my mother and father and bring them to stay with us. On the way to Nicosia we saw Cypriot tanks on the main road. The roads were not suited for them and so the tanks caused a lot of damage to the asphalt. This made it very difficult to drive in our Morris Minor 1000 car. A Cypriot army officer stopped us and wanted to know what we were doing. We did not know whether they were for or against Makarios and so were very careful in our explanation. We simply explained that we were going to pick up my elderly parents who were helpless in Nicosia. I had to do the talking as Robert's broken Greek would cause many to think he was Turkish. That would have caused us difficulty in this situation. They let us go.

When we got to their house, we saw them sitting there waiting with their packed suitcases. They did not know what to do and seemed shocked at the whole situation. When they saw us, they cried. Robert and I calmed them down, we had a coffee together but set off back to Larnaca soon after. We put a French flag on our car aerial to indicate our neutrality. This, we thought, would reduce our chances of being targeted. After we came back to Larnaca, we left our house again but this time for the Dhekelia base where we thought we would be safer. At the Dhekelia base, Harry had arranged our sleeping quarters in the cinema that Robert worked in. We had two rooms on the first floor of the cinema allocated to us. We had the projection room and a second room next to it, which thankfully had air conditioning. It was not a luxury hotel but under the circumstances, we were very happy to have the space. Harry had kindly set up camp beds in the room. I noticed mice running around which made me shiver but I was still glad we were there. The five of us stayed there from early August until early September. If we needed something, we could go back to our Larnaca house. I remember going back a couple of times to do the laundry. Harry and his family had space for themselves on the ground floor of the cinema. He had his wife, two young sons and his mother with him. His two sons, Yervant and Mihran would play with Baret. Both Robert and I would go to work while at the Dhekelia base. My parents would look after Baret during the day. Harry would bring food from the garrison mess and we would eat together in the evenings. When Robert put on the movies for the people in the cinema, we would sometimes go and watch too. I remember the auditorium was very smoky and not good for Baret so we did not go too often. We felt safe in the base. When we could, we would go to the beach for relaxation. We had our car so getting around was easy and apart from the fact there was a war on, in many ways it was a sort of nice holiday. We would go to the Cessac beach restaurant, which is still there at the time of writing. Today it is called the Lambros Fish and Chips Restaurant. From there, we would watch helicopters carrying supplies from the distant British cargo ships to land. The British had organised supplies for the refugees. Robert filmed all this with his camcorder. He also filmed the refugees in the camp queuing for food.

The British Base was divided into multiple camps to house the Cypriot refugees. Our camp was called the Anzio Camp. The thousand British soldiers that would normally populate the camp moved out to enable the two thousand or so refugees to move in. Many of the refugees were staying in tents under trees or in their cars. The ones with British passports used the nearby airfield to catch a military flight to England. We saw other Armenians that we knew had ended up there too. I remember seeing the Ouzounian and Sultanian families. They were very well known in the Armenian community. I did what I could to help by taking them lemonade, food and clothing. I was able to use the NAAFI supplies shop to purchase what was needed as I worked at the base. The refugees were not permitted to shop there. On the BBC Radio, I heard the Turks had taken Kyrenia. There were reports of looting and rape. The Cypriots were fighting not just the Turkish invaders from the northern coast but also the various Turkish enclaves around Cyprus where the local Turkish Cypriot forces had retreated.

I spoke on the phone with my English friend, Nannette, who lived in Famagusta. She was married to a Greek Cypriot and called me wanting advice on what to do. I had heard rumours about the Turks planning to take Famagusta and I advised that she leave immediately. I told her to use both of their cars and with her husband to come to Dhekelia, making sure they take their valuables. I told them it maybe drastic but that they could always go back if the enemy did not take Famagusta. Thoughts of leaving Cyprus started entering my mind. I could not live in a Cyprus overtaken by Turkey and so seriously started thinking about what I could do. I spoke with my boss at the BFBS about this and he said: "Don't leave Cyprus as this is how far they are supposed to go." Meaning they had taken Kyrenia and the parts of Cyprus north of the Attilla Line. He did not want me to go. He said: "The worst is over, why go now." Then, on 15 August, the Turkish forces went into Famagusta as the Greek soldiers pulled back. My boss growled: "Bastards! They were not supposed to go that far!" It was almost as though there was some agreement as to how far south they could come and they had gone beyond that pre agreed limit.

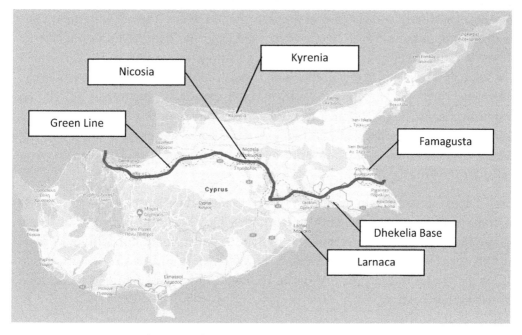

Map of Cyprus indicating extent of Turkish invasion in 1974

As this unexpected move meant the Turks did not respect an unofficial agreement with the British, I thought this must mean they could move in anywhere. In fact, there were reports that the Turkish military were moving towards Larnaca. The Greeks in particular were very scared and spread such rumours. Luckily, my friend Nannette had taken my advice and moved out of Famagusta just before the Turks overran it. Nannette and I had had many conversations over coffee in the past. I had told her my mother's stories and how cruel the Turks had been to her in the past. She would say I was prejudiced and would remind me how Germany had bombed England but that now they were all friends. The English had forgiven them and they were even trading together. She said we Armenians should do the same. I pointed out that Germany was officially at war with England at that time. In the case of the Armenians, none of this applied. It was pure and simply Genocide with the Ottoman Turks turning on their helpless Armenian citizens. Now that Turkey had taken her home in Famagusta, she told me how much she now disliked the Turkish invaders and apologized for calling me prejudiced. She had only lost her possessions, which could be replaced. She acknowledged my mother had lost her family that could not be replaced.

The British were not getting involved militarily against the Turkish invasion but were concerned the Turks could turn against them. As a precaution, the British brought in Gurkha fighters from Nepal to support the British in such a scenario. These Gurkhas were small in stature and very sweet natured. Robert would interact with them a lot. He once offered them a nice bottle of ice-cold water he had cooled in the cinema fridge. In return, they gave him hot chilli peppers they had with them. Robert would give some of the chillies to my mother who really liked them. The Gurkhas would call the chillies "glir" and Robert and mother would chuckle to themselves as "glir" in Armenian means "penis". I have to say I was disappointed the British would need support from the Gurkhas. I always thought of the British as being a superior fighting force with no need for such support. However, the Nepalese soldiers had come to look after the British soldiers.

After things settled down and the Turks stopped their encroachment in early September, we decided to go back to our house in Larnaca. Our suitcases were still packed ready for our now overdue trip to Beirut. We stayed there with my parents for the next few days. These few days, however, were pivotal in my life. It was during these days that my gradual desire to leave Cyprus turned into a firm decision as I will explain next.

Leaving Cyprus

When the Turks invaded Cyprus in 1974, they took one third of the Island in a matter of weeks and then stopped invading further. I was 34 years old at the time with a young son and elderly parents to care for. I had just gone through a most terrible experience not knowing if I would live. People around me feared the Turks would restart their efforts and take the whole island under Turkish rule. I was especially fearful as I knew about what the Turks had done to my mother's family years earlier. I felt that I had to leave the beautiful island I was so fond of. I had to get my family out of Cyprus. My many conversations with my mother instilled an underlying fear and mistrust of the Turks. I remember how during the most horrific parts of her story, when her parents were murdered, I would be angry with her and say: "Why didn't you retaliate and fight back. Didn't you have any weapons?" My mother would go quiet and say: "You don't understand my dear. We were helpless and could do nothing."

After we left the Dhekelia Base and went back to our Larnaca house, I remember having a heated conversation with my mother. We were talking again about her childhood and again I was being angry with her for not putting up a fight. She took the opportunity to tell me off and show me what it feels like to be helpless at the hands of the Turks. She said: "That fighting talk is all fine if you are not in the actual situation yourself. Will YOU fight now? The Turks are at YOUR door now! They have the knife at YOUR throat now! What can YOU do! NOTHING! You are helpless like I was!"

The exchange was heated and I responded: "I will not unpack my bags. I will go to England instead. When I go I will not come back." Out of her anger, she dared me to go to England. That was the spark that ignited my plan to get out of Cyprus and go to England. My mother was very upset with me. But not just me. She was upset with the whole situation and in particular the Turks. Because of them, she lost her childhood. Again, because of them she will lose her daughter to England.

Robert did not want to leave Cyprus but I convinced him. We agreed to leave Cyprus and start a new life in England. I discussed leaving and going to England with my very kind boss at the BFBS. He reluctantly agreed to let me go saying for my son's sake that I should. He warned me the rainy weather in England will not be to my liking. He also told me that he will keep my position open for three months should I change my mind and come back. We also discussed the matter with Robert's less caring boss. His reaction was: "You are both Armenian, what difference would it make to you if a Turkish government took over. To you, they are both foreign." He obviously did not know about the painful history between the Armenians and Turks.

Over the next few days, we packed several suitcases of our belongings for England. The rest of our things had to be sold or stored. We stored our furniture and homeware in an area of the house we used for general storage. However, that was the last we saw of our chairs, tables, cutlery and plates. They were soon stolen and we would only find out when we returned a few years later. My favourite item was a musical table that played the Blue Danube when you opened the drawer – I missed that most. I gave any food supplies to my sister Yeghis. We had a lot of food as we had stocked up when we thought there would be a war. We also left my pet cat, canaries and rabbits to her. My brother's wife Anna found a buyer for two of my beautiful rugs, she managed to sell them for £120. Robert put this cash in his pocket and it turned out to be very useful, as I will explain later. We sold our car, I remember, for £400. This cash was in the form of a cheque, which we would need to cash when in England. Even aside from the emotional reasons, getting out of Cyprus was not easy in 1974. Due to the imposition of emergency regulations, we were not permitted to take more than £150 out of the country per person. Therefore, we could take a total of £450 for husband, my seven-year-old son and myself. With this small amount of money, we had to travel by ship to Greece, take an overland train through Europe to Paris and then another ship to England. We had to pay for all our travel fares, accommodation and other expenses. Nicosia Airport was bombed during the invasion and so there were no commercial planes able to fly out of Cyprus. All maritime activities had also been suspended. Eventually, in September, Greek ships started to sail from Limassol and this was the only way we could get out. Due to the high demand, we had to pay three times the usual price to get on one of those ships. Even so, we did it. We set sail from Limassol on 8 September 1974. There was only one thing in my mind: "I am going to England and do not need to worry about the Turks anymore."

The ship was overcrowded and it was difficult to move around. There were people everywhere: in the corridors and on the deck. With great difficulty, we managed to store our luggage in our cabin and then go on deck. We stood there watching Limassol in the distance. With my son's hand in one hand and Robert's in the other, I said: "I hate this Island. Thank God I am leaving. I will never go back!" Suddenly I heard my little boy's trembling voice: "But what about grandma and grandad!" He started crying and I suddenly realised how selfish I was being. I was leaving the rest of my dear family behind. We stood there in silence for a while. Tears ran down my cheeks. Eventually I managed to say some words: "As soon as we get established in England, we will bring grandma and grandad to live with us."

Robert, Baret and Margaret in 1974

Part 2 - My Journey to London
Limassol to Athens

How can I ever forget this journey. Our plan was to get to Athens by sea and then to catch a train through Europe to Paris where we would stay with Robert's family for a while. Although his family had moved to Cyprus, they moved back to France when Robert's father died in 1967. We would then head across the English Channel to London. My cousin Serpouhi Manoukian had kindly offered to put us up in their home until we were able to sort ourselves out. We had eleven pieces of luggage with us. When the ship docked in Greece, we stored the bigger items at the train station as we had some time before our train was scheduled to leave a few days later. One of the bags was very heavy and contained my gold and silver jewellery. We took extra care of this one as it was so valuable.

I had been to Athens before and had stayed at the hotel El Greco. We went straight there by Taxi as I had a good experience previously. My niece Shoushig had befriended a young man called Herman while they were both students at the Melkonian Institute in Cyprus. After graduation, she remained in Cyprus but he had moved back to his hometown of Athens. Seeing our situation, she told me we could phone him and that he could help us while we were in Athens. We did so. Herman came to our hotel with his family and they took us out for dinner. We told him we were leaving in a few days by train to Paris and he promised to come again and see us off.

That evening my son Baret had a bad stomach-ache. It seemed serious to me so we took him to Accident and Emergency at a nearby hospital. There were many people there waiting to be seen and we had to wait our turn. I could see this was going to take a long time and could not bear the agony on my son's face. I managed to arrange to get the doctor to see him more quickly by going private and paying for the service. The doctor was very nice. He said Baret's pain was due to his anxiety about the situation. He gave Baret some medication after which he felt much better and started asking when grandma and grandad were coming. Robert and I thought we should go to a cafeteria to get his mind off things and lift his mood. We ended up in a very posh restaurant with waiters serving while wearing clean white gloves. We hesitated to go in for a moment, thinking this will cost us a lot of money that we cannot spare now. A waiter approached and asked if we wanted a table for three. As we were tired and just wanted to sit down somewhere we went in. We were conscious about our casual dress and apologised telling him we were refugees from Cyprus. He apologized the Greeks were not there to help and beckoned us to a table. He said: "Let us at least welcome you to our restaurant". We had very little money to keep us going so I planned to have something small but I wanted Baret to have whatever he wanted.

The owner came to see us after we sat down. He brought us drinks and said it was on the house. He asked about the situation in Cyprus. We told him we came by boat and that we had been away for a week so we do not know what is happening now. We could not keep in contact with my family very easily as calls were very expensive. We did talk a bit about the military planes sent by Greece that were shot down by the Greek Cypriots in a tragic case of friendly fire. The Cypriot Military had no aircraft and so Turkey had complete air superiority. Greece decided to support the Cypriot fighters by sending troops on several Noratlas transport aircraft but they had not communicated this properly. As a result, the Cypriot anti-aircraft gunners fired at them thinking they were Turkish planes. We were all in tears for a very long time. He looked very sad. He shook our hands and wished us good luck. On the way back to our hotel, we saw a shop for kids. I really wanted to ease Baret's trauma and so said to Robert: "Let's buy some clothes for Baret." Robert was not keen as we needed the money but again I managed to convince him. Later that evening we spent some more time with our new friends, Herman and his family.

On the day we were to depart by train, we had a hearty breakfast at the hotel. We took a taxi to the station. Found the platform and got on the train. Ten minutes before departure, Herman came to see us off. He asked about our luggage that we had put into storage. It suddenly dawned upon us that we had to take them out of storage and put them on the train – the company would not do that for us as we had assumed. In a panic, he rushed to the storage area and retrieved the luggage in time. In this way, we saved our luggage. He also gave us a big box of baklava for our journey. We did not know at the time how important that would be. We had no food on us as we thought we would buy what we needed on the train. We were so wrong about that.

Train through Europe

Come evening, the train was overcrowded. Passengers were forced to stand in the corridors due to lack of space in the cabins. To take Baret to the toilet, I had to push my way through the crowds. It was very unpleasant. Robert also had to push his way through to get around. He went looking for a shop selling food and drink but there was no such shop on the train. He did find out the train would stop for a longer period in Rome allowing an opportunity to buy food there. As we were very hungry, we opened the box of baklava our friends from Athens had given us. Robert and I each had one but Baret did not like it. I tried to get him to eat it but he was not interested. Robert had a few more.

We then tried to sleep. Baret slept on my lap and Robert on my shoulder. I carried on looking out of the train. My mind went back to how things were like in Cyprus. I thought about how we moved out of our rented accommodation to our first newly built house. How we decorated it the way we wanted. How we bought the new furniture. How wonderful Baret's bedroom was. How happy he was at school. I thought about our cat "Minu" and our two beautiful canary birds in their cage. How Baret loved to play with Minu and feed the birds. How we planted a rose bush in the garden and Baret looked after it so well. I remembered the first rose he brought to me from there. I was so surprised that he had done that at such a young age. When he had done this, he had also pricked his finger and I had put a plaster on it to stop the bleeding. Outside we had two beautiful white rabbits. Baret loved them. I thought about our work and how happy I was working at the BFBS. During that time, Robert worked very hard but was content that he was able to earn a living and support his family. Then I thought about the day when Robert was at the BFBS Radio Station with his sound recorder. He was there as a guest while I was translating Greek songs to English and explaining their meaning on the show. The first broadcast of this type was so successful the public listeners wanted more. I was excited about this. Alas, it did not last. The happy thoughts came to an abrupt end when I then I remembered the first Turkish bombings which happened as we were recording on that day.

My focus returned to the train. I looked at my son and husband both sleeping in the uncomfortable conditions. I wondered if we were doing the right thing leaving. I started getting hot flushes from that moment and have not stopped getting them since. I felt the responsibility on my shoulders, as I was the one that pushed us to leave our home. Robert and Baret did not want to leave but I made it happen. Now I was having doubts about whether it was the right thing to do. I thought I had to leave Cyprus due to the physical and mental problems I was experiencing. Whenever they mentioned the Turks coming to Larnaca, I would have a panic attack. As I could not sleep, I started to think ahead to our future life. About going to Paris and meeting my mother-in-law, Ida, again. I would see Jacque, Robert's eldest brother, Silvie his wife and their kids Patrick and Isabel. While deep in these thoughts, the train suddenly stopped.

The Greek train crew left and the Yugoslav train crew boarded. We were now about to enter Yugoslavia. A ticket inspector with a very stern face approached and asked for our tickets and passports. On inspecting Robert's passport, he said: "You out!" This is because Robert had a restricted British passport which did not permit him to pass through Yugoslavia without a visa. We had no idea he needed such a visa. Our plan was to go to Paris, not to stop off in Yugoslavia. As Baret and I had a full British passport, we were permitted to go through. Robert tried to explain that he was not planning to get off in Yugoslavia, and that he was only passing through on his way to Paris. He stated a visa is not needed for passing through but his bluff had little chance of working. The guard was getting impatient and said even more forcefully: "Out!" On the realisation he was going to be forcibly removed from the train and separated from us, Robert got emotional. In tears, he beseeched the passengers near us to help me to get to his brother in Paris. In our cabin, we had befriended five very nice French University students that were going to Paris and they assured Robert they would help and that he should not worry. As Robert made his way off the train, I quickly picked one of our suitcases at random and handed it to him. Unfortunately, it was the one containing all our winter clothes and did not help him at all. I was left with the remaining ten pieces of luggage and a seven-year-old boy to look after. No food or water. It was the first time I saw my husband cry. I also wanted to cry but I held the tears back thinking about Baret and not wanting him to be even more frightened. I sat there as the train pulled away without Robert. Baret did not ask for anything to eat or drink and just sat there. He sat on my lap until my legs went numb.

We heard Greek music coming from the adjacent cabin. The singer was talking with the friendly French students. They must have told him about us because he came over to see us. He said to me: "I am Mikis Theodorakis. I hear you are a refugee from Cyprus." He could see I had been crying and continued: "Please don't cry anymore. I am sure your husband will be fine. Once he gets his visa, he will be able to join you. Do you know what happened to me?" With a sad voice he said: "I was thrown in prison by my motherland Greece. They said I was a communist because I was writing politically provocative songs. They excluded me from Greece for a time. I am on my way to Paris too." I did not know who he was at the time but realised later that Mikis Theodorakis is a major figure in the recent political history of Greece. He is probably most famous for his composition of "The Syrtaki Dance" which was the theme tune to the movie "Zorba the Greek". He was also politically active and in 1967, the right-wing Greek Junta government of Greece saw his left-wing influence as a threat. They banned his music and exiled him. He had connections in France, having studied there years earlier, and managed to fight against the Greek Government from there. Eventually in 1974, he was able to return to Greece and continue his political activism as well as his musical career. We had room in our car and so he came and sat with us. He spoke in French with the students and in Greek with me. The boys got him to translate something they wanted to say to me. They said they would phone my brother-in-law when they get to Paris and they will help me carry my luggage off the train. They would not leave me until I am safe with my brother-in-law. I thanked them for their kindness in my very limited and broken French.

Robert, having grown up in France, spoke French very well and befriended them as we started our journey in Athens. Robert had got on very well with them. They were on their way back to France after going for a kibbutz in Israel where they worked picking grapes for a winery. I talked with Mikis a little about what was happening in

Cyprus. He then told me how bad things were for him in prison. He said that after his ordeal he thought he would never go back to Greece. I said: "I don't think I will ever go back to Cyprus." He played a few sad songs on his guitar that were not familiar to me. He told me they were protest songs. Then he played a few that were familiar to me and we all enjoyed his entertainment.

Suddenly the train stopped. I did not know where we were but it must have been a scheduled stop at a station somewhere inside Yugoslavia. It was an opportunity to get something to eat. I asked the French boys through Mikis, who was now my acting interpreter, if they could get some water and a sandwich for Baret. They came back with water and two sandwiches. I had only asked for one. I gave them some money but they did not accept it. Baret and I did not even look what was inside the sandwich we were so hungry. I thought back briefly to how Robert was optimistic we would get a bite on the train and how disappointed we were when we realised this was not possible. We were also disappointed at how crowded the train was and how uncomfortable it would be to travel such a long way in just a seat. We had planned to upgrade our ticket to get a couchette. That way we would have a small sleeping cabin and be much more comfortable. However, that idea vanished when Robert was thrown off. The sandwich was delicious. I ate only half of mine thinking we still had a long way to go and Baret may get hungry again later. I also saved some of my water.

Soon it got dark. The corridors were full of Yugoslavs and I had to push past them again as we made another toilet trip. When we returned, I asked Baret if he wanted the half sandwich that I saved but he did not. I thought maybe I could give it him for breakfast in the morning. The lights were lowered and Baret went to sleep without brushing his teeth. During the night, I noticed Baret was making sudden jerky movements. I thought he having a nightmare at first but then I realised the Yugoslav guard was poking him with his baton so he sits up. Baret was lying partly on Robert's empty seat and partly on his own seat. The guard had noticed he was using up two seats and so was trying to vacate Robert's seat so someone else could sit in it. The lights were dimmed so I could not see very clearly but then realised what the guard was doing. I also recognised him as the same guard that threw Robert off the train. I was enraged and yelled at him: "What are you doing to my son you stupid man!"

He said: "Boy sit straight, Yugoslav sit here" in his broken English.

I said: "That is my husband's seat, the one you threw out at the border."

He said, again in broken English: "No speak English".

I said: "I don't speak Yugoslav".

One of the French boys saw what was happening and said that was his seat. He sat down for a moment until the guard left. He then left the cabin and then said in his limited English: "Don't worry, I am just outside the cabin sitting on your luggage so they don't steal it." I thanked him. I then tried to sleep but I could not. This was the second night in a row I could not sleep.

In the morning, things were a bit better. As we passed into Italy, the guards changed again. The more joyful Italian ones replaced the rude Yugoslavian crew. We were now in Italy. I gave Baret the other half of my sandwich and water that I had kept. He said, thoughtfully: "Let's share it, mum."

I said: "No. I prefer to have some Baklava – you know how much I love it." I was so proud of how thoughtful Baret was.

I started thinking about Robert and what he was doing. Was he safe? Was he hungry? I began to cry again. The boys saw me crying and told me, via my translator Mikis, that we are stopping in Rome and that they will get more food and water for me. I was crying mostly because it was all my doing. I was the one that made us leave Cyprus for England. I felt guilty.

It was time for me to take Baret to the toilet again. The corridors were not that busy anymore. We washed our faces and used the toilet paper to dry our faces. I no longer cared if anyone stole my handbag or belongings. When we got back to our seats, one of the kind students was looking after our things. He asked if I was OK in English. I was not OK but told him I was and thanked him for looking after our things. I was going through a lot of pain but as there were people around that cared, like the French students and Mikis, I had hope. Their kindness gave me strength and I am very grateful for that. Mikis was there and with a smile asked me what sort of music I liked. I told him a few that came to my mind. He sang one song after another. He had a lovely voice. Baret was very interested in his guitar. Mikis showed Baret how to play a few notes. Baret could not speak Greek so the conversation was very limited. At least he was entertained for a little while.

I looked outside. The Italian scenery was breath taking. The lake was blue like the sea and I had never thought there could be so many shades of green. I forbade myself to enjoy the moment, however, as I did not know what my poor husband was going through. Hours went by and the train eventually stopped. The boys told me we were in Rome. They asked if I wanted anything in particular. I told them I would like a basic sandwich and some water again. We stopped for only twenty minutes but that was enough time for the boys to bring the items. They came back with salami, cheese, French bread and a small bunch of grapes. Baret gobbled up the grapes in no time. In Cyprus, where in the summer grapes were plentiful, he would have eaten twice as much in one go. We shared the beautiful bread, salami and cheese. We also kept a bit for later. The boys gave me some wine in a plastic cup. I did not want any but Baret said he wanted some so they gave it to him. I offered the Baklava. They all had some but we still had more – it seemed never ending which was great. Mikis had some too and commented how delicious they were. I offered some money for the food but they would not take it and said: "We provided the main course and you provided the delicious desert." I thanked them again.

Baret was bored so we played I spy as we used to play in Cyprus when we went on long car journeys. We used to regularly travel between Larnaca, Nicosia and Limassol in Cyprus in our Morris Minor and so we would play a lot. We entered France and it began to get dark again. I could also see how tired Baret looked. We went through the toilet routine again and came back to our seats again. The lights were turned down low. As the weather was getting cooler, I put my jacket over Baret and he went to sleep. I began to cry again but I told myself that things would get better in the morning because we would be in Paris. We were going to see my brother-in-law and I was sure he would have news of Robert. In addition, we would finally be able to take a shower and get into fresh clothes. Those thoughts did bring a smile to my face. I said a silent prayer and kissed Baret as he slept. Again, I could not sleep. After some time, I could see the sunrise. It was lovely. A new day had started and we would soon be in Paris and our ordeal would be over. We had bread and cheese for breakfast. Baret shouted: "Keep some for later on."

I said: "Good thinking Baret."

As we approached Paris and our time together was coming to an end, Mikis said to me: "I don't know where I am going and you don't know where you are going. I have no address to give you so we can keep in touch. Maybe you should follow my music. I know you will be alright. You are a beautiful and bright lady." I thanked him for his kindness and he moved on to deal with his luggage. Then we pulled into Paris station.

Paris to London

The French boys got our luggage out from the train. They helped me with Baret and tried to telephone my brother-in-law Jacque but did not manage to get through. Suddenly I saw Jacque. He rushed to us with open arms. He said: "Don't cry you are home now. All will be back to normal."

I turned to the French students that helped us so much and thanked them yet again. Jacque looked at them with suspicion. I said to Jacque: "Please thank them for looking after us so well."

With great difficulty, he said: "Merci." I could see, however, that he was not happy at all. I can understand because he was very old fashioned. He did not like the idea of a young woman being with five young men. I never got to know their names but they were very kind young men and hope God blessed their lives after we parted.

A few years previous Jacque had come to Cyprus for a holiday. We took him all over the island in our Morris Minor. We visited Kyrenia, an Armenian Monastery and numerous villages. We had a great time and got on really well. Jacques was very much a father figure to me and I felt I had known Silvie, his wife, all my life though we had only just met. When they left Cyprus, we missed them dearly and so I was looking forward to seeing them again. Their children were so disciplined and I regretted not being able to speak French so I could get to know them better. Jacque took us to a very old flat where his mother, Ida, and his very old father-in-law, Mr Kilimyan, lived. Ida, though was old herself, would look after Mr Kilimyan who was very old. They were both very serious people. I told Baret to be extra nice to them. I asked Ida if Robert had phoned. She said: "Yes, but he couldn't get a visa from where he was. He had to go to Athens to get the visa."

Unfortunately, he was very far from Athens. Jacque had told Robert to get to Athens and then fly to Paris, which would mean he would not need a visa. After a week and enduring many difficulties, he got to Paris. After he was thrown off the train at the Greece/Yugoslavia border, a local Greek man saw his predicament and helped him. This man allowed Robert to stay at his home in Thessaloniki. While there, the man's fiancée washed Robert's clothes for him and fed him. The man also helped Robert buy a plane ticket to fly from Thessaloniki to Paris. Thankfully, Robert still had the £120 cash that my sister-in-law gave him following the sale of our rugs. This was just enough to cover the cost of the ticket. At Paris Airport, he got off the plane wearing shorts that were clearly in need of a wash. As Jacque went up to him to help him with his suitcase, Robert joked: "Let me carry the suitcases – that way I can pretend to be the porter and not think about my poor state." We laughed and cried at the same time as we had an emotional reunion.

When we got home, he said he needed a shower. This was not as simple as getting in the tub and turning on the hot water tap. Robert had to put firewood in the boiler and wait until the water had heated up. Normally they would do this once a week and everyone would bath the same day but Robert broke the rule that day. That meant Baret and I also benefitted with a bath sooner than planned. It was very good to have Robert back with us. He helped with Baret and he also helped his brother with his work. Jacque had a shop in St Germain where he sold underwear. He also had a space at a local market where he would also sell the underwear on Sundays. Robert would help him with whatever was needed, loading and unloading the van etc.

Baret was finding life in the flat very tough. He was not allowed to speak aloud or run after his little toy car. He was told off all the time. He kept asking when grandma and grandad are coming. Annoyed at the delay, he abruptly said to me: "If they can't come, you can send me back to them in Cyprus!"

It was understandable for the old people to have these strict rules as they were set in their ways. They would eat at a certain time and sleep most of the time. I was very grateful for their help in giving us a place to stay but their ways made it very hard for us. Silvie, my sister-in-law, could see what was happening and found the solution to our problem. Every morning she would come and take us out to see the sights of Paris. That way, we would not have to be in the flat that much. We went to the Palace of Versailles, the Louvre and many more places. Whilst we enjoyed this, we found everything very expensive: the tickets, drinks, sandwiches. If we did this once in a while it would be OK but to do so every day it was tiring and too expensive for us. We brought our own sandwiches from home to economise and that helped a little. Going out was very good for Baret. He enjoyed being out in the fresh air. This also meant that when we would eventually get back to the flat he would be more relaxed.

At night, the family would get together for dinner. Most of the time it would be rare beef steak. Baret would not eat it and Uncle Jacque would say: "You must eat it. It is very good for you." Discreetly, Baret would push the steak to my plate and in return would eat the accompanying chips from my plate.

One day we had a call from my father's cousin Serpouhi. She had found out we were in France and wanted to see us. She visited one afternoon. Her family had a knitwear factory. She had lost her husband and was living with her eldest son. She also had a chauffeur that would drive her to us and wait outside until she wanted to go somewhere else. She was a gentle soul. She was just like the main character from the 1989 film Driving Miss Daisy. She brought knitwear for Baret, Robert and myself. Over tea, she was thinking over how she could help us. She said she had a beautiful chateau and that we could go and live in it for as long as we wanted. She urged us to find a job and stay in Paris. She said her son would help us in any way he could. He was very well established. This was encouraging but our plan was to go to England so we thanked her and said we would think about it.

Another option for us was to remain in the old flat with Robert's family. As Robert had options for work as a plumber, it would be a matter of time before we would be able to afford our own place. Another consideration was buying a restaurant in a village on the road half way from Paris to Deauville. We visited it based on information from Jacque. It was beautiful and in a great location near the seaside. It had eight rooms for us to live in too. The decoration was very old French design with beautiful red and white gingham curtains and tablecloths. We loved it. Baret went and found his bedroom to be and a room for grandma and grandad. The problem with staying in France, however, was we could only get access to my substantial severance money from the BFBS in London. The arrangements were for the money to go to London. At this time, there was no easy communication with Cyprus so making changes to this arrangement would have been almost impossible. We were fast running out of money and really needed to get access to the significant sum that was due to me. Staying in France was also a problem from a language point of view as neither Baret nor I spoke. I did study French at the Likion College in Cyprus for two years but was not at all fluent. Robert did speak at least.

One night after dinner, we were sitting in the lounge. I had a call from my cousin Serpouhi Manoukian from London (not to be confused with the other Serpouhi that was my father's cousin). She wanted to know why we were still in Paris and said we need to be in London sorting things out. Before leaving Cyprus, we had arranged with Serpouhi that we would go and stay with them. She was expecting us but did not realise how long it would take us to get there. We left Cyprus on 8 Sep 1974. We reached Athens and stayed there for 2 days. We then caught the train through Europe, arriving in Paris 4 days later. However, we stayed in Paris for 3 weeks instead of heading straight for London. Serpouhi convinced me I needed to get moving and head for London to sort things out. She pointed out that I had many letters that arrived for me from Cyprus "On Her Majesty's Service". Mail received in this way was not the usual postal mail. Due to the issues in Cyprus, normal mail was disrupted but the British Military would still deliver mail using their military network. As I worked for the British, my mail took this route. I had letters from my boss from the BFBS and from my brother Garbis who also worked with the British at the base in Akrotiri.

I told my cousin Serpouhi that we would soon come to London but that we will have a lot of luggage with us. She said not to worry as she and her husband would come and pick us up with their van from Victoria station. We decided that I would initially go with Baret to work out what we can do in London and if we liked it. Robert would stay for a time in Paris working and earning money. He said if I did not like it, I should come back to Paris. Otherwise, he would come over too. It was very difficult to say goodbye to Robert but we had to do it. Once more, I was alone with Baret. The journey, however, was much better as we had plenty of food and water. We made sure of that!

My cousin Serpouhi and her husband Hagop were waiting for us at Victoria station. The journey from there to their house in West London was very long. There was a lot of traffic. More than I had ever seen in my life. Serpouhi said it was the rush hour but that it is not always this bad. Finally, we got to their house in Ealing in the evening. It was cold and wet. I remembered what my BFBS boss had told me about me not liking the cold and wet. He was right. I thought Baret must not catch a cold and fussed over him so much about that. He caught a cold anyway. He then got better but then caught another. I nursed him all the while and eventually I think he got used to the English weather.

We arrived on a Friday in mid-October. The following day we went out greeting various people including Haig Bedrossian, who was the best man at our wedding. When Haig saw me wearing my heavy coat, the only coat I had, he joked: "What will you wear when the weather gets really cold!" I had no answer to that.

Hagop and Serpouhi, our hosts, had some guests over at the weekend and so we got to meet more Londoners. One of the reasons for coming to London was the family we had here. My father's brother, uncle Zareh was here. His son Haroutyoun lived in Earls Court with his family. His daughter Serpouhi was in Ealing and I had just moved in with her and her family. Serpouhi was my older cousin who also happened to be my teacher when I was at the Melikian School many years earlier. I remember her being one of the few teachers that were kind to me and would take the time to explain things rather than tell me off. My father's sister, Chrissy was also living in London. Her son, Michael was living in Chiswick with his family. Her daughter, Flora, was living in New Malden with her family. Haig Bedrossian, the best man at our wedding was also living in Ealing. His wife had died in Cyprus and he was rebuilding his life in London. At this time, he was helping his brother, Kegham, relocate to London with his family. I also had many school friends here but did not get to see them until much later. I did not realise it at the time, but due to disagreements, the families were not on good terms with each other.

Monday arrived and they advised me to register with a job agency and not lose any time getting a job. It was raining very hard that day and in Cyprus that would have meant staying indoors. I said: "I don't think we can do anything today as it is raining cats and dogs." It rained from morning until the following morning. My cousin, Serpouhi, said: "This is how it is in London. You will need to get used to using an umbrella."

Hagop drove me to Chiswick in his Jaguar car. It was a very short journey and I thought to myself getting around is not so bad. I was previously worried that I would get lost trying to get about in London by bus or train. It seemed a much bigger place than Cyprus. He dropped me at a recruitment office called "Josephine Sammons". He explained that to get back I would need to catch the 91 bus back to Boston Manor Road. He then left. The agency took my details. I had not yet officially left my previous job and was officially on a 3-month leave. I was determined not to go back, however, so I spoke frankly with them and told them of my situation. They understood and quickly found me an interview then and there. They sent me to Wimpy's head office which wasn't too far away. I had to walk for fifteen minutes in the rain. I was drenched even though I had an umbrella. I was conscious of how terrible I must have looked as I turned up. I asked the receptionist for a Mrs Garside. "Yes Mrs Karakatounian, she is expecting you". I was ten minutes late and not looking my best and so was concerned I was not going to make a good first impression. But I was determined to do my best. Mrs Garside took me into her office. We talked for a while and got on well. She told me about the role at Wimpy. Wimpy was a famous fast food restaurant franchise and my role would be as a receptionist at the head office. Here they would receive customers from all over the world that were interested in the Wimpy franchise. My ability to speak Greek and Turkish would be very useful as a large number of customers would come from Greece and Turkey. These customers would come to negotiate their franchise and receive training on starting up running a Wimpy franchise.

I told her about my previous role at the BFBS and all about the regimented nature of the place. We talked about how people would dress in Cyprus and that while hot pants had become very fashionable, there was no chance we would be allowed to wear such clothes in a formal office environment. In fact, women were not permitted to even wear formal smart trousers. She explained the vacancy was for a receptionist role working under her and that she was the Personal Assistant to the general manager. Then she introduced me to David Achison the General Manager. "This is Mrs Karakatounian who is very suitable for the receptionist position. She also speaks Greek and Turkish just as you required." With a smile on her face, she joked: "In her last job, the dress code was such that she could not wear hot pants". He smiled and shook my hand confirming the job was mine. "Take your time about getting yourself sorted out and come into the office to start next Monday." I was over the moon and could not believe that I got a job so easily. In Cyprus, getting a job was certainly far more difficult.

Friends had warned me about a culture shock when moving to England. I thought that was all rubbish as I was always working with the English in Cyprus. Even my boss in Cyprus had said that my command of the English language is excellent. I thought I had nothing to worry about in this regard. To my surprise, things were different in reality. It was very difficult as there were so many words and phrases that I just did not understand as I had not been exposed to them. Also, there were many words that I thought were English words but were not. On my way back I went to buy some fruit from the green grocer. I asked for "an oke of apples", a phrase used commonly in Cypriot markets where English was spoken. The "oke", however, is a Turkish unit of weight used in Cyprus at that time. One oke is about 1.3Kg. I did not realise at the time, however, that this was not an English word. The green grocer mocked me for making up words. "The lady would like an oke of apples!" he said loudly in a fake posh voice and laughed away. I did not understand why they were laughing but later realised that I was speaking English and using foreign words without realising. Anyhow, I got my fruit and carried them home in two plastic bags. That meant I could not use the umbrella. I needed a third hand. I did not care anymore and got wet. I found the 91 bus and went home.

I told Serpouhi and Hagop about my new job and they were very happy for me. They agreed to sort out Baret's school enrolment, as I now had to be at work. My new job also prevented me from taking Baret to school myself. However, I was satisfied that Hagop and Serpouhi would take care of him. That night when Robert phoned from Paris, I told him about my job and that he must start planning to come over. We got Mr Gulbenkian, an Armenian immigration lawyer, to work for us to get Robert his UK residency so that when he came over he could work.

Robert asked: "Are you ok? Is this what you really want?"

I could see he needed confirmation and so reassured him: "Yes, come as soon as you can."

I now started looking for a place of our own to live. Having a child did not make this very easy. It was very difficult to find somewhere to rent with a child. I tried every avenue but nothing worked. I went to multiple estate agents but as soon as I mentioned I have a young son, their faces would drop. They explained landlords were not keen on tenants with children as they had more legal rights should a dispute arise. I also was looking to buy, but I could only do that after I was a resident for 3 months with a building society account.

Every night when I got home from work, Serpouhi would ask if I found a place. I would say no and would feel very bad as I was dependent on her and Hagop. It looked like I would need to burden them for longer than I was planning. I had been there for 2 weeks already and there seemed to be little chance of us moving into our own place any time soon. The main problems were time and my lack of knowledge of the area. I worked Monday to Friday with only a 45 minute lunch break. Then I had to go home straight after work to take care of Baret. This meant I did not have any time during the week to see a place. Even if I had managed to arrange a viewing, I could not easily visualise where the various places were and how I would even get there. Hagop did take me to see a few at the weekends but they did not work out. My very old aunty Chrissy advised me not to say I had a child. She suggested I could explain his presence later by saying he came over from Cyprus. However, that would be lying and I just could not do that.

While I was looking for a place to live, I was also trying to get Robert a visa to come over to the UK. Mr Gulbenkian, our lawyer, said I needed to have five thousand pounds in the bank to prove that we will not be a burden on the government when Robert came over. By this time, I had sent my formal letter of resignation to the BFBS and was waiting for my severance pay, which was several thousand pounds. This sum eventually came through via military mail. I was also getting money from my brother Garbis in the form of cheques also sent via military mail. Soon after, I received a letter from my old boss at the BFBS saying: "I am very sorry that you are leaving. BFBS's loss is Wimpy's gain. Do come back and see us when you next visit Cyprus." Again, I cried a little as it made my move feel more permanent. However, I could not cry for long as I had many things to do.

Robert came to England a few days later, in early November 1974, using his French identity card. Within a week, he found a job with Rank Audio Visual in Brentford not far from where we were staying. He worked as a technician repairing damaged electrical equipment rejects. In this way, the company could salvage some of their losses. He came over on a 6-month visa but we were engaging with Mr Gulbenkian to extend that. It was so difficult living from a suitcase. Robert and I shared a single bed in the box room of the house. To get to open the suitcase we had to shuffle things around the room. Baret was on a camp bed in Vartan and Samuel's room (Hagop and Serpouhi's kids). On weekdays, it was not as bad as we would all be out. However, weekends was another story as we would all be in the house and it got very crowded. I was getting very down about finding our own place and not being able to move out from my cousin's house. Mrs Garside, my boss, found me crying at work. I told her about the situation and she was very sympathetic. She said: "This afternoon I will be working only for you to find a place to rent."

Later that afternoon, she came down to reception where I worked. She said: "Take this £20 note and map" as she handed me the money and map. "Go and put down a deposit on it immediately. Don't waste any time calling your husband to arrange a viewing or it will most certainly go."

It was in a very nice area of Ealing called Fairlea Place. Ideal for Baret's schooling. I went and put down the deposit but they wanted a guarantor, which Haig Bedrossian agreed to be. Haig congratulated me and went on to say his mother lives opposite Montpellier School that Baret would go to. He very kindly said Baret could go and stay with his mother until I could pick him up after work. Robert and I were so happy we finally had our own place. After staying at my cousin's place for a month and a half, we moved into our own two bedroom flat on the weekend in early December 1974. We went to second hand shops and bought things we needed to furnish the place like beds, a fridge and a cooker. My cousin Michael, God bless his soul, brought us a bed for Baret and some blankets. He took us shopping for food. He said: "We will come and check on you and help in any way we can."

Because of our move, Baret had to wait until after Christmas to start at the new school. Therefore, Baret missed school for one month. The month he could not go to school, I had to leave him with my Aunty Chrissy while I was at work. I woke him up at 5:30am, dressed him, made his breakfast and took him by bus to Ealing Broadway Station. From there we took the underground to Chiswick and then walked to aunty Chrissy's house where he would be looked after during the day. I would then walk from there to my Wimpy office to start work. I was allowed 45 minutes for my lunch break. In this time I would take sandwiches for my aunty. Baret and I would not have time to sit and eat together. After work, I would go to pick up Baret. On the way, I would pick up some food from Marks and Spencer but had to be quick as they would close around 5:30pm. I would then go back to Ealing the same way, cook for the family and look forward to going to sleep and being ready for the next day. I always loved Friday nights as I would sit down with aunty Chrissy and talk about life over coffee with her. Then on Saturday and Sunday I would catch up with all the neglected house work. Robert, however, worked non-stop including overtime at the weekends. He did this for several years so we would have a chance at a decent life in England.

After moving into our new flat, our first electricity bill came and it gave us a shock. The £350 bill was unexpectedly high and worried us. As our combined monthly incomes was not enough to pay it, thoughts of how we need to economise even further went through my mind. I said we should cut down on food so we can afford this amount. Haig Bedrossian came to see us and we discussed our bill. He said there is definitely a problem and the amount was unreasonably high. He said that on Monday we will go together to the utility company office and he will see to it that it is corrected. It turned out the people before us in the flat had used the electricity and we were being charged for their usage. I was so relieved when the bill was reduced to less than a third.

We did not yet have any chairs in our flat to sit on so we looked around for some furniture. Unfortunately, everywhere we went they told us there was a lead-time of several weeks for deliveries. This was a problem for us especially as it was almost Christmas. In Cyprus, Christmas would be a family affair. We would always go to my parents in the early days but then in later years we would mostly have a party at my house in Larnaca and invite family. My brother and sisters would always be there and we would have a great family Christmas. We were now in England with no immediate family so would be experiencing something different. I noticed how much colder it was in London. The fact that houses in England were better insulated, however, meant that indoors you would be much warmer. Our flat had underfloor heating and we loved it. We would sometimes lie on the floor to feel the warmth. We had a colour television in the flat but did not really have time to watch it much. I spent most of my time running around getting things done. I was preparing either the evening dinner or the following day's lunch for Baret and Aunty Chrissy or something else. At Christmas, however, I found a bit more time and remember really enjoying watching the British shows like Bruce Forsythe's Generation Game. I liked them much more than what they showed in Cyprus.

One Saturday, the women in the neighbourhood took me for a coffee and we had a nice chat. I told them about our difficulties with Christmas just around the corner. They said they would like to come to us for a Christmas day house warming drink. I really enjoyed their company but did not want them to be disappointed at our lack of the basics like chairs to sit on or tables to rest their drinks. This was not a problem for them and they said they would bring us a few items they no longer needed that we could make use of.

On our first Christmas, Robert had to take two days off work as Rank Audio Visual was closed for the holidays. Christmas morning I prepared some nibbles and placed them on the kitchen worktop. Robert had brought some nice wine from France that his brother had given him. Four couples came with their own chairs and tables that they would leave for us to use. They also brought drinks and deserts. Their generosity and kindness moved me and we had a wonderful time. We had bought Baret a cassette player as his present and he was happy with it. That was Christmas day 1974.

When Baret started school in January 1975, he would come home before I came back from work. As such, he had to stay home alone for nearly two hours after school every day. As he began to learn the language, he told his teacher he was scared about being on his own and that he would hide under the bed until I got home. He had the key to the front door on a chain around his neck. To add to his troubles, at that time, some children would regularly bully him as he made his way home. To appease them, once in the house, he would throw chocolates to them from the window. This would appease them for a while and they would leave him alone. On one occasion, while my niece Ani from Cyprus was staying with us, the usual group of bullies surrounded Baret. Ani saw this, called out to Baret from a distance, and thus rescued him from his tormentors.

The teacher asked him: "Why does your mother work?"

Baret replied: "If mother doesn't work we will go hungry."

Not long after that, I received a letter from the headmaster to say he wanted to see me. I went in and found him very polite and considerate. I asked: "Is there a problem?"

He said: "Yes but I think we can get it resolved." He went on to ask: "Are you unable to make ends meet if you didn't work?" I had never heard the term "make ends meet" and asked what he meant. He said: "You know you may qualify for child benefit." At this suggestion I was very upset.

I said: "I will never be a burden to the government. I promised that when I came to England."

He said: "You will only be asking for your rights. Anyway, leave it with me. We will sort this out."

He found a woman that had recently retired and lived in a building very close to us. She was willing to look after Baret for two hours after school. I was later told that I could have gone to prison for neglecting my child. I also heard stories of how social services have taken away children from their parents in similar situations. I thought to myself "what was I thinking!" Once more, I can say there were good people looking out for me.

Robert was working very hard. He never took a day off. He worked every weekend as they would pay him extra then. Life was very difficult with him working all the time. I had to do everything else myself and mostly during my 45-minute lunch break. As we were so busy, we did not realise until a week or so before the due date that Robert's 6-month visa was ending and we had still not secured an extension. Even to the last day we still did not know whether Mr Gulbenkian, our lawyer, had managed to secure an extension or a passport for him. I was so worried. I knew that if he did not get extension, he would have to go back to France before coming back again for another 6 months. This was permitted under the European Economic Community rules. I also knew that going to France and coming back would take some time. He could not afford that time away from work and would mean he would likely lose his job. Jobs were very hard to come by at that time and we really needed the money. I followed up with phone calls to our lawyer and the Home Office trying to find out why we had not yet heard from them yet. Mr Gulbenkian made enquiries to push our case through. It was now the day before Robert's visa ended and I was getting desperate. I phoned Mr Gulbenkian with a lump in my throat. I asked: "Does Robert have to go to France in the morning? Please tell me what we are to do in the morning."

He said: "I am in contact with the Home Office and will call back with news in half an hour or so."

The next 30 minutes felt more like 30 days. The phone eventually rang. I jumped to the phone and held it tight in case I dropped it. He said: "Are you ready for the news?"

I said: "Yes! Yes! Yes!"

He said: "The decision is that he can stay. I will post the relevant documents to you."

I was so happy and relieved. When Robert came home that evening, he was exhausted. He had waited 20 minutes for the bus only to find that it was crammed full and so had to wait for the next one. As he was elaborating on his horrible journey back, I interrupted him and said: "Hush! Guess what? You can stay in England!"

He said: "How do you know? Are you sure?"

I told him about my conversation with Mr Gulbenkian and what he had said. "Robert, you don't have to go to France in the morning!" Baret was also there and the three of us hugged each other very tightly. We must have gotten carried away because Baret asked us to stop as we were hurting him and that he could not breathe. We let him slip out from our hug but the two of us continued until we went numb. I was extra happy as it was because of me we were uprooted from an established life in Cyprus. Slowly but surely we were getting established in England. A few people were helping us. This was a big step.

The terms of our tenancy stated three people would be living in the flat but soon after we had guests to accommodate. Ani, my niece from Cyprus, came to stay with us in early 1975. She came to study in London. Then in the summer of 1975, my mother also came to stay for several weeks to look after Baret during the summer holiday. I was concerned about violating the terms of my tenancy but the chairman of the building, who would have known about the extra people, was very kind and did not say anything to us. When my mother came for the first time in the summer, she remarked how Ealing was like the Troodos Mountains in Cyprus – a little cold and very green. She did everything to support us. She paid her own flight to come to England and, when here, she would economise on electricity. While we were at work, she would switch it off and only turn it on when we got home. I know because Baret would complain that when he came home from school the house would be cold. Mother used to tell him that young people do not need heat. That they are hot enough. Boy could she cook. She would provide so many lovely dishes with half the ingredients I would use and still tasted much nicer. In between cooking and washing up, she would undo my old pullovers and knit for Baret so he did not feel the cold as she would put it. We all enjoyed my mother being with us. She spoilt us and it was so hard at the end of the summer when she went back.

The other person I will not forget who showed me so much kindness was my very kind friend and boss Muriel Garside. I do not know how I would have coped without her. I thought that since I had my mum looking after us and my wonderful boss on my side, I could go for my next challenge. This was to buy a house. Muriel found me a solicitor and pointed out suitable areas. Robert and I saw about six houses. Robert did not like any of them as they needed a lot of work. Robert was a very hands-on person and was capable of such work but as he worked so many hours, he did not have the time or energy. My knowledgeable cousin Michael advised me to go for a more substantial house. He said that even if it were not in such great condition it would prove to be a wise investment over time. However, I had to compromise given our situation. I also had in mind that Robert was reluctant to buy anything because it was a risk. In addition, we had a financial incentive to stay in the flat. If we lived there for five years, the housing company would give us several thousand pounds. This was written in our contract. I could not wait that long and in the longer term buying was a better financial decision. I calculated that house prices would rise and leave us unable to afford a house altogether if we delayed. One day we went to see a house in Ealing and I fell in love with the garden roses of every colour. I thought I was in heaven. I said I want this house and, as it did not need much work done on it, Robert liked it too. So we bought it and moved in. It was April 1976.

Prior to buying, we were five people living in our two bedroom flat. Ani was with us all through 1975 and then in December 1975, my brother Garbis also came to live with us. Garbis had temporarily left his family in Cyprus to enable him to find a job in England. It was a huge step for him as well. It must have been hard for him to leave his wife and three boys for several months while he did this. My mother said to me that she could sleep better at night knowing that my brother was here as well. She said that we should look after each other. She made me promise and I did. I said: "Have no fear mother, we will look after each other."

In the old flat, Ani and Baret shared one of the bedrooms while Robert and I had the other. Garbis had the living room. It was very crowded but then we got the 3-bedroom house and for a short while had some extra space. After a couple of months in our new house, however, we had more guests and were short of space again. Garbis was now ready for his wife, Anna, and his three wonderful boys to come over. He had secured a job and was in a position to have them over. They came to stay with us in June 1976. As the saying goes, "the more the merrier." We persuaded Garbis to also buy a house. At first, he was worried about overextending himself financially but then he went for it and found a house near ours. This way we were close enough to help each other. They moved into their new house in February 1977. It was very hard when they left. The house felt empty. On the other hand, I am so glad he bought the house. The prices went up significantly the following year.

My cousin, Michael, was advising us a lot at the time. He was urging me to buy and also for Garbis later on. He would say that property will increase in price and will be out of our reach if we did not act soon. He was right. In 1975, we paid £13k for our

3-bedroom terrace house in Ealing. The same house, a couple of years later, would have cost us double that. We were very lucky. The prices rising so much, however, meant that it was impossible to buy another house for my father. He wanted to come and be with us but due to the financial situation in Cyprus after the Turkish invasion this was very difficult. No one was buying or selling there which meant he could not get the capital together. Even if he could sell his house in Cyprus for a decent price, he was only allowed £1000 out of the country. Following the ceasefire agreements, this was the rule. I said they could come and live with us but mum wanted her own place. She said she wanted to live next door to us. Sadly, that was not possible.

Ani finished her studies and went back to Cyprus. Not long later, her brother Haig came to live with us. He was starting his studies in London. He stayed about a year and half before finding his own place. The years went by. We went to see my parents in Cyprus and they came to see us in England. Each time we parted, it was very difficult. The first time we went back, Robert saw the political situation was still unsettled and said he was glad we made the move to England. This lifted a huge burden off my shoulders. Up until then, I carried guilt for turning his life upside down and making him move here against his will. In his mind, he thought things in Cyprus would settle down and we would go back. Now, he did not want to go back. I did not want to go back either. Even today I do not want to go back there to live. My guilt for leaving my parents and not being able to get a house for them in London remained, however.

Part 3 - My Parents' Genocide Stories
1992 Interviews

In the early years, after we moved to England, my parents visited us every year. As they got older, however, they found travelling more difficult so we visited them in Cyprus more often.

One year we fulfilled my father's dream of visiting Armenia. I knew what it meant for my parents to visit Armenia and wanted to take them for many years. While I was in Cyprus, however, I could not go due to my work. My BFBS contract stipulated I was not to visit a communist country or be a member of any communist organisations. After my move to England, this no longer applied so in 1987 we went. Due to evening curfews, we would get together in various hotel rooms for small parties. As we drank and had watermelon we bonded with the group we travelled there with. We also sang a lot. My father loved to sing and had a good voice. He was having the time of his life. During the day, we visited various historical sites. I will never forget how my father's face lit up when we went to Echmiadzin, the headquarters of the Armenian Apostolic Church. He stretched his arms out and prayed the Lord's prayer out loud. I had tears in my eyes as I could see how much this meant to him. As we walked through the churchyard, he called me excitedly as he spotted the site where Khrimyan Hayrig was buried. He said: "When I was a child living in Soloz, Khrimyan Hayrig's death in 1907 was big news. There was 3 days of mourning for this great saintly priest. He was dearly loved by the people." Khrimyan Hayrig was the Armenian Patriarch of Constantinople. He was one of the most influential Armenian leaders of the time, looking out for the interests of his people in very difficult circumstances under Ottoman rule. His real name was Mgeurdich Khrimyan but the people affectionately referred to him as Khrimyan Hayrig ("Hayrig" being the Armenian word for "daddy"). I must comment on our experience of the communist system that nearly spoilt our trip. You can forget about the level of customer service we expect in the UK. Going through passport control, we had to stand on our feet for well over an hour. This was too much for my elderly parents but the Soviet officials at the airport did not care. We almost had a fight with them to get them a couple of chairs for them to sit on. At one point, my father got sick and needed medical care. The hotel doctor, with his rusty stethoscope, examined him and determined he needed an enema. For some reason he expected me to perform the enema! Many of the local Armenians we encountered did not take a liking to us. I worked out that they thought we were spoilt brats from the UK and that we were looking down on them. That could not be further from the truth but we could do nothing about it. Overall, however, the trip was a success and my father would not stop thanking me for taking them with us. They were in no position to go by themselves but having them with us made the trip extra special for me.

Robert had bought a camcorder from Rank Audio Visual where he worked. He enjoyed recording special family occasions and took it with us to Cyprus when we went there in 1992. We went to visit my parents and decided to record them as they told their stories. After a nice lunch together, Robert and my father had an afternoon siesta while I sat on the veranda with my mother for coffee. My mother was again telling me of her childhood days. This time she was very angry. She said: "It was bad enough what they did to me then but now they have taken my daughter away too. When are they ever going to stop?" She meant the Turks that had committed the crimes against her when she was young had also separated her from me by invading Cyprus.

Robert and my father eventually joined us for coffee and that was when I said to Robert: "Why don't you record my mother's story. That way we will have a record for Baret and one day he can watch it." Keith Rawlings, the program producer back in my days at the BFBS in Cyprus, had planted this idea in my head many years ago. He had even written down a number of questions to tease out my mother's story. I remembered the words he used to describe the possibility of bringing their memories to film: "Now that would make one amazing story!"

With great difficulty and many pauses my mother started telling her story to the camera as Robert filmed her. Poor mum cried a lot and her blood pressure went up while re-telling and so re-living her horrific experience. After the recording, she was not well for days. We also took the opportunity to record my father's horrific story. He spoke well and remembered a lot of detail for the camera.

As we were getting ready to return to England a few days later, my mother called me to her room. After every visit, she would be sad and bring up the fact that I left her. This always made me feel very guilty. When I walked into her room, she had such sad eyes. With a trembling voice, she said: "Use the recording to tell the world what happened to me and my family and I will forgive you for leaving us behind." I promised her that I would. I could not look her in the face as I felt such guilt. I was supposed to be her mother, father, brother and sister all in one. Now when she needed me more than ever, I am so far from them. I felt like I had betrayed her and I had to live with it. My mother always wanted to make her story more widely known but she was afraid of reprisals from the Turks and also lacked the expertise. She was not the type to use technology like camcorders or to write at length. Perhaps she thought with my drive and relative safety in England, the opportunity was there for this to happen.

My mother had a stroke in 1994 while she was alone in the garden. She fell on the floor and lay there for several hours until my father eventually realised she was not around and went to look for her. He managed by himself to drag her into the house and get help. She then had to go into care as she was unable to walk. In early 1995, she moved into the Armenian Kaladjian Rest Home in Nicosia where she got professional care until her death on 21 October 1995. After living alone for a few years, my father needed a hip operation after which he went to the same care home. On 16 January 2001, he also passed away. We buried him in the same Armenian Old Cemetery in Nicosia as my mother.

I know my parents loved me but were disappointed that I left them for England. I know at times they looked at this rationally and could see good reasons for how things turned out. It was good that we managed to get away from the war and uncertainty in Cyprus. It was sad that we did not manage to relocate them to England to be near us. I also sense, however, that sometimes they looked at what happened less rationally. In these moments, they looked at things from a purely emotional perspective. When looked at that way, I was guilty in their eyes for leaving them when they needed me most. I also felt guilty, as I wanted to do so much more for them. If the odds were not stacked against me I definitely would have.

During the First World War, the Ottoman Turks saw an opportunity to get rid of the large Armenian population from the lands under its control. Armenians were a large minority population living in villages and cities within the Ottoman Empire. There were other large minority populations like Greeks and Assyrians and they have their own similar stories. This arrangement was due to the expansion of the Ottoman Empire into previous Kingdoms including the Armenian Kingdom that existed from the time of the Romans.

Many Armenians were relocated at the start of the war "to protect them". In practise, however, this was a successful attempt to rid the land of Armenians. The Turkish authorities collected the young men that could provide physical resistance into the Ottoman army and put them in labour camps. Most of them died there. They then collected the intellectuals and influential leaders and murdered them. The date this happened was 24 April 1915 and Armenians commemorate this date all across the world. On this date, each year, Armenians remember what their families went through and what the Ottoman Turks did to them. After murdering the leaders, the remaining Armenians were the women, children and elderly. These were now defenceless and voiceless. The authorities forced them to leave their villages and towns and made them journey to other villages saying this was for their safety. The intention, however, was for them to be murdered. The murders were arranged, in many cases, by allowing prisoners free and encouraging them to attack the Armenians.

For a time, the Armenians were forced to march long distances to live in government-provided homes in villages far from their homes. They experienced many hardships and attempts on their lives during the period from 1914 to 1918. One and a half million Armenians were murdered during this time. After 1918 when the war ended, some of the Armenians that survived returned to their villages for a time. They were then subjected to a further threat, that of Mustafa Kemal Ataturk. In 1918 Turkey was a beaten force and was about to be overrun by the Greeks and Europeans. Ataturk, who became the leader of the Turkish people, caused them to rise up from this situation and was encouraged to do so by France and Russia. This was due to the political agendas of the great powers of the time. That meant many Armenians were again forced to leave their villages and this time it was for good. You will see what this meant for my mother and father as I now tell their stories.

Nouritsa's Story

The story that follows is my mother Nouritsa's account of the horror she went through as a child. It covers the time from her early childhood until she got married. Robert recorded her on video as she told this story in Armenian. I then translated the words she spoke into English. Here, you will see the transcript transformed into a more easy to follow narration that includes things she had told me over the years.

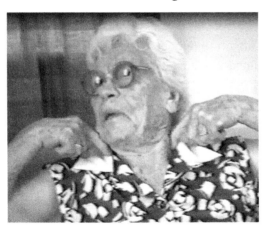

Nouritsa Kiremidjian telling her story in 1992

Nouritsa's earliest memories were very traumatic as she witnessed the worst of the Armenian Genocide. As the Ottoman Turks burnt down many Armenian schools, churches and homes at the time, Nouritsa did not have an official record of her birth. This, and the fact that she was an orphan from a young age, meant she had no way to know her exact age. She estimated, however, that she was born around 1910.

Although she was very young at the time and did not understand all that was going on around her, she pieced together the stories through what she saw and what her older sister explained to her.

When Nouritsa was a young child in the village of Gurden, the Turks came and murdered her mother, father and two of her brothers. Her older sister was forced to marry a Turk so that she was not murdered also. Nouritsa was adopted by a kind Turkish couple that looked after her well. After the war ended, she was collected from her Turkish parents and reintroduced into the Armenian community. Due to the rise of the Turkish leader Ataturk, the orphanage that looked after her had to close. They did, however, manage to get her to the safety of Cyprus where she lived the rest of her life.

Genocide Begins

Before 1915, she remembers living in peace and regularly reading her prayer book in Turkish. Turkish was the language she knew, not Armenian. She would learn Armenian many years later. Her father was Garabed and mother was Elsa. She had four brothers and one sister. In age order they were: Mihran, Alexan, Mesrob, Nazely and Melkon. My mother, Nouritsa, was the youngest. Mihran, the eldest brother, was away in the army when the horrifying events in 1915 started. Her only sister, Nazely, was married to an Armenian. She was in the early stages of pregnancy when her husband also left for the army at that time. The family were poor farmers. Their means of a living was their barn animals and the land which they would work to produce food.

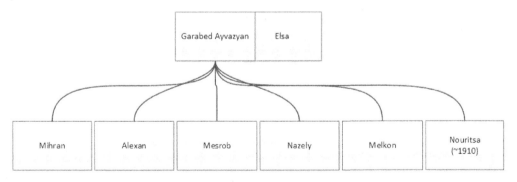

Nouritsa's family tree

One day in 1915, the Ottoman tax collectors came to her village of Gurden in the area of Yozgat to collect their contributions of wheat on behalf of the government. They took their share of the harvested wheat in their horse-drawn cart. At that time, the Ottoman authorities would heavily tax the minority populations within the empire. As Nouritsa's family were Armenian, this meant they were taxed at a much higher rate than their Turkish neighbours. This caused a lot of resentment among the minority population. As they were leaving, they stopped near a bridge and let their animals free into a field to feast and do their business on the wheat still growing there.

Anna, Nouritsa's sister-in-law, was riding on a horse towards the field where the rest of the family were harvesting their crops. On the horse with her were my 5 year old mother and Anna's infant daughter. The plan, as usual, was for my mother, Nouritsa, to play with her infant daughter when they got to the field. This would leave Anna free to work. As she approached the bridge, Anna noticed the tax collectors' horses roaming around the field damaging the crop. She exclaimed: "How terrible that someone would do such a thing. Look at the state of the field with crops damaged and animals pooping everywhere."

On hearing this, an angry voice from under the bridge responded: "You are travelling nicely to harvest your crop. This is the government's need. What do you think – our animals don't need to feed too!"

Sensing danger, Anna whipped the horse to get them out of there. She eventually reached the field and, as planned, my 5 year-old mother looked after the infant child while Anna started work alongside her father and brothers that were already there. Not long after, a cousin rushed over and with an urgent message from the village mayor. He shouted: "Something serious has happened in the village. It is relating to the mayor's son. You have all been instructed to come to the village immediately. You must not do any work and just come immediately to the village. The situation is very bad."

It was the time of the First World War and there was already news filtering through about what was going on all around the Ottoman Empire. The Armenians and other minorities were under suspicion and were being treated badly by the Turkish authorities. Garabed, Nouritsa's father, responded: "They want to draft me and my sons into the army! I will come but give me some time to collect the wheat we have been working on. If we have to go away, at least the women and children can use the wheat to make bread and have something to eat." At that time, the poverty they lived in meant food was very hard to come by and working the field was necessary to be able to eat.

The cousin said: "No you must come immediately."

So they all hurried back. When they got to the village there was a big commotion. The mayor's son had been found murdered. The Armenian villagers were angered, shouting, "They did this!" Meaning the thugs that the authorities had let loose to intimidate and murder the Armenians. The Turkish police had come from the nearby village on their horses. They made a big fuss about catching the perpetrator for the terrible crime. The Armenian villagers thought these expressions of outrage from the police to be a pretence. They believed there was no real intention to stop the crimes committed against the Armenians. They were right as much worse followed.

Mesrob Murdered

Not long after the mayor's son's burial, a wealthy Turk from a neighbouring village came to talk business with the Mayor. Many in the Armenian community, again, took this as a pretence that the Turks were trying to get along with their neighbouring Armenians by doing business. They strongly suspected the Turks were planning to cause them problems in the near future. Some in the Armenian community wanted to appease such people in the hope that they would look upon them more favourably in the event of troubles breaking out. The wealthy Turk asked: "Is there someone in your village who has lots of children that I can take back with me to look after my children?" It was common in those days for a wealthy person with young children to "buy" an older child from a poorer family. This would help both parties by unburdening the poorer family of a mouth they had to feed and at the same time provide a nanny for the wealthier family's children. The Mayor introduced the Turk to my grandfather, Garabed, but he said: "Sorry I cannot. I need all my children with me."

The Turk then said: "How about if I leave a hundred of my sheep with you. You can look after them, milk them, make cheese, and make butter. The ones that die – you can take the skin off and make leather. Whatever you produce, half will be yours and half will be mine. There is no money to be exchanged. Do you accept?" Again, this was a show. He knew the men would be officially drafted into the army very soon and would not be able to carry out their part of this bargain. In fact, he likely knew that the men would be murdered rather than be allowed to join the army. Garabed naively thought this a good offer and was keen to appease the Turk. He discussed the deal with his son, Mesrob, who was a shepherd. However, Mesrob did not agree to do the work of tending the Turk's sheep. He knew his intentions were not good and that trouble was coming. He also did not think that appeasing the Turk would serve them any benefit. Garabed asked him: "Why don't you want to do it?"

"Father", said Mesrob "What they have done to the mayor's boy, they will do the same to me."

"Oh my son!" said Garabed, "You are looking for a reason not to do it."

The wealthy Turk, on hearing of Mesrob's refusal, said "I can see this is not going to work out. It is better that I take my flock of sheep away." He took them and went.

My grandfather, Garabed, collected the remaining villagers' sheep and told Mesrob not to disappoint the villagers at least. Mesrob was uneasy about going out alone during these times but reluctantly agreed to go out for the smaller flock owned by the villagers. He told my grandfather he would take them out at night time but not during the day. He said: "At night I am not frightened, father it's the daytime I am frightened."

After Mesrob left that night, my grandmother Elsa decided to send her youngest son Melkon to be with him. She put food and blankets on a donkey and said: "Melkon my son - go and stay with Mesrob your brother. He left angrily and that is not good. Please just for tonight go and sleep alongside him."

Elsa followed Melkon for a time and saw, from a distance, that he had caught up with Mesrob. They were together in a deep valley with a stream in the middle. The two spent the night out there on a hillside field. In the morning, Mesrob told Melkon: "Return home with the blankets, I will lower the flock to the stream so the animals can drink water." Melkon left. Mesrob, now on his own, lowered the flock to the stream. At this time, my grandfather Garabed and his son Alexan were out early harvesting the wheat. Garabed was suddenly overwhelmed by an unexpected feeling of grief and had to take a deep breath. Alexan, noticing his father's strange reaction asked: "What happened? Are you OK?"

Garabed replied: "Oh Alexan my son, something happened to my heart and my whole body feels strange."

"Oh father", said Alexan, "They said to you to stay in the village but every day you come here and bring us here to work on the fields."

My grandfather Garabed replied: "What am I supposed to do! They need food back in the village."

Soon after, news came that they had taken the shepherd, Mesrob. "The shepherd is gone! The shepherd is gone! The shepherd is gone! And all the flock are also gone!" The villagers searched and searched but found no trace of Mesrob.

Again, the Turkish police officers came and made a fuss. Using foul language, they said if they caught the person who did it, they would do this and that. My grandmother Elsa, the poor thing, just cried. Later some Turkish people from another village came saying there was good news.

"What do you know?" asked my grandmother.

"We found your boy!" said one of them.

"Where is he?" pleaded my grandmother.

"In Urimdiou village. We found him near the police station. He was sitting there on a street corner. We asked him 'What are you doing here?' He replied: 'I don't know, the authorities thought I was eligible for being an army recruit and so they brought me here. I have older friends and brothers in the army but I am still too young. Why did they do this to me?' I told him: 'I will sort this out for you but first I will send news of your whereabouts to your mother so she doesn't worry. And so I came here to tell you. Will you send anything to him? Will you send clothes? Will you send food? Will you send money?"

My grandmother Elsa said "Why didn't you just bring my child back?"

Another said: "Tomorrow at this time, the authorities will come here as well. They will recruit all of the young men and take them as soldiers. What would have been the point of bringing him here only to be recruited again and taken back?"

On this barely plausible story, my desperate grandmother prepared some bread and boiled eggs. She gave the items over to the men so they can give them to Mesrob. Then they went.

In the evening, another Turk came to my grandmother and asked if she was Mesrob's mother. "Tomorrow, around this time, I will bring your son back here." he said.

My grandmother desperately wanted to believe these men, but the poor thing was being deceived by them. In this way, they managed to get material goods from her and play a sick joke on her at the same time. This went on for several days.

During this time, their sheep dog would come and then disappear for a while before coming back again. My grandmother, Elsa, eventually noticed the dog's strange behaviour and remembered the dog used to follow her missing son Mesrob everywhere. Elsa thought to follow the dog. She took a Turkish woman and my mother, Nouritsa, with her. The dog led them through the fields and to the water mill. They found his dead body there. He just lay there with cuts all over with the wind blowing his hair and torn flesh around. They had dumped his body there after murdering him. The poor boy. It was as though his body was a big lump of coal. Near that place, they had a field where they would grow beans. My grandmother Elsa, and the Turkish woman got some dry grass from there. They then dug a hole and filled it with the dry grass. They dragged Mesrob's dead body by the hands into the hole and covered it with soil. That is how they found Mesrob. With the help of their sheep dog.

Men of Gurden Murdered

Several days later, the authorities came to their village to take the men away. My grandmother, Elsa, was still mourning Mesrob's death as she went about her daily work. She was making some bread when, Alexan, came and said to her: "Stop thinking about Mesrob and start worrying about us. Mesrob is already dead. We are alive but are about to murdered as well!" My poor grandmother did not know what to do or think anymore. She had just found Mesrob dead and now they were going to take away her husband and other son Alexan! The authorities said they were recruiting for the army. They took my grandfather Garabed and his remaining adult son Alexan. They also took the other men from the village. They rounded them up into the church saying this was so they could be formally conscripted into the army. They collected rope from the houses and used it to tie the men up. Their plans quickly became clear. They were not being conscripted, they were about to be murdered! The women of the village voiced their horror and questioned the need for them being tied up. The authorities, still keeping up the ridiculous pretence, replied: "What business is it of yours how we get these men into the army!" They beat any woman that protested and interfered with their process. After tying them up, they marched the men out of the church. They beat any that marched slowly. They marched them to another part of the village and massacred them there.

A few days later, the authorities came for the older men. My great-grandfather, who had a long priestly beard, was made to sit on a donkey along with the other elders. They took them away to meet the same fate as the younger men. My great-grandfather shouted and protested as they lead him away but he could do nothing. That is how my great-grandfather was murdered.

They then said to the women and the children that were left: "Go and bury your dead." How could the women bury all those people and work the fields to feed themselves? They decided not to bury their dead. Because of this, the authorities piled the dead bodies in a large pit and covered them up. The people that did this to my mother's village were not the local Turks. The authorities brought Kurdish prisoners into her village and they were the ones that did this.

Women Re-Marry to Survive

They did not harm the women and children. The authorities said they would be taken to various villages so they could learn to become Turkish. Of course, they already knew the Turkish language but they would also teach them the Islamic faith. They would teach them the Islamic prayers and customs so they would "become" Turks. They said they had to go to these villages. They had no say in the matter. While the authorities were deciding where to send them, Nouritsa's pregnant older sister, Nazely, escaped with her three sisters-in-law and mother-in-law to another village. This is the sister who was married to an Armenian soldier that was already away at war at this time. A crazed Turkish man, Ahmed, who they knew from their village, went after them. Ahmed was a deserter from the army. He was already married with multiple children but had his eye on Nazely. This was his opportunity to get her for himself. He managed to find them in the other village. While they were asleep, he grabbed Nazely by the hair and pulled her out of bed. He then raised a sword to her and said: "Either you marry me or I will kill you". At the time, women were treated as though they were the property of men. The crazed Ahmed was exerting his "rights". The other women pleaded with him and got the landlord involved to leave Nazely alone. Nazely, however, accepted his marriage demand as she feared for her life.

Ahmed came back alone to Gurden looking for my grandmother so he could break the news. My mother's family had a large garden. In it, they had tall cannabis plants and he walked through them to get to the house. It was common in those days to roast the seeds of the cannabis plant and eat as a snack. Nouritsa could hear his footsteps: "ksher ksher" as he approached the house. My young mother was home alone eating the bowl of yoghurt soup that my grandmother had prepared for her. My grandmother had told Nouritsa: "By the time you eat this I will have gone to your aunt's place and come back." My great-grandmother and numerous great aunts lived nearby. Nouritsa could hear the footsteps coming towards her from the garden: "khsher khser khsher." She was frightened that someone would come into the house and started to cry. The man came out and said: "Don't be frightened my little girl. I am going to look after you really well. I have become your brother-in-law. From now on there is no more death for you. Do not be frightened. But where is your mother? Go and get her." This was now the pretence side of Ahmed coming out. He forced Nazely to marry him in such a barbaric manner and was now making claims that he was doing good by protecting them with his Turkish citizenship. Nouritsa ran to my grandmother saying: "Mother, mother, someone has come!" She was frightened, thinking they were in danger. Nouritsa told her about the man and what he said to her about marrying her sister. My grandmother went home to find Ahmed. When he saw them, he said to my grandmother: "Don't worry, I am now your support and no more harm will come to you."

My grandmother was growing ever more tired of the horror she was enduring. She replied: "I *wish* harm would come to me! What's the point in continuing to live now that my husband is dead and my sons are gone?"

New Born Murdered

Not long later, the authorities told them they had to go to the other villages. This was part of their plan to "Turkify" the nation. They were preparing to deport them to the other Turkish villages. They brought horse-drawn carts and loaded my mother's family and other Armenians onto them with their few belongings. Nazely was now married to a Turk, Ahmed, and so did not need to go. The authorities provided them with information about who was going where. Some families would go to one village and other families would go to another village. Then they set off to the village they were assigned. My young mother was with my grandmother, her sister-in-law and Melkon. They stayed there at the village for a while. After a few months, some of the other Armenians with them decided to leave and go back to their home village. Then another family went back and another and another. The Turkish leaders of the village reported this to the authorities, explaining how so many

Armenian families that were sent to them are not listening to them and simply returning to their home villages. The authorities responded by telling them to let them go. Of course, their intention was to massacre the Armenian women and children who resisted "becoming a Turk". The events where the villagers were returning to their original villages must have been about one year after the time when men were murdered.

As no one was stopping the villagers returning to their homes, Nouritsa's family also went back. For a time after they returned, no one bothered them. No police came to their house and no Turk troubled them. They thought this was strange but then thought maybe this was because they were thought to be part of Ahmed's family. Nazely was now in labour with the child from her original Armenian husband. Ahmed said to her: "I already have 5 daughters from my other wife. I do not want another. I will have the child killed if it is a girl. If the child is a boy, however, I will keep him." The child was born, and it was a girl. Ahmed said: "You will not feed the child. No milk, nothing. This baby girl will die."

With Nouritsa's and her sister-in-law's help, they managed to look after the child secretly for a few days. They hid the child from Ahmed. They would take cow's milk and pour it into the child's mouth. However, the baby would cry continuously. The crying was within earshot of Nazely who would cry herself in her room. They had an Armenian neighbour who had married a Turk to survive these events. She came over and said: "The child will die whatever you do. Let her die quickly and so not suffer. This way your suffering will not be prolonged either. Put some hashish mixed with milk into her mouth so she dies quickly. Otherwise you are going to suffer as well."

After getting agreement, she put the mixture into the baby's mouth. For 3 days and nights, the baby made whimpering noises but then gave up her spirit and died. After the child died, the neighbour tried to get my family to bury her corpse but none of them had the strength to do it. As they were too traumatised, the neighbour buried her. Sadly, the horrors did not stop there.

Women of Gurden Murdered

Soon after, the authorities came and collected the Armenian women that refused to adopt the Turkish culture. They collected the women to murder them just as they had done a year ago to the men. At that time, my grandmother knew what was coming. She would be murdered and her children would either be murdered or taken to be raised as Turks. As the crazed thugs approached, she hid Nouritsa under the floor of the house. She then hid Melkon under some hay in the barn. She told both her children that she would also hide somewhere and so they should not worry. She loved her children but she was so traumatised and broken that her intention was to kill herself. She could not do anything more for her children. A kind Turkish man, who was a neighbour of theirs, intercepted my grandmother as she left to go to her death: "Elsa my dear, you do not need to die. Stay and marry me. Become my wife and do not go. Let me rescue you." He appeared genuinely to care for her. The Turkish villager was one of many such men who got along well with their Armenian neighbours before these troubles. They were not part of this horrific act of genocide perpetrated by the authorities. As such, they did what they could to help in the circumstances.

"What are you saying!" said my grandmother. She was so traumatised and full of emotion and did not react to him kindly even though his intentions were good. "To me, a Turk's body has the smell of a dead dog. I would rather die than marry you. I have to go. I have to go." She did not listen to the man that was trying to help her and went. Nazely went running after her but my grandmother was resigned to her fate. She cried: "Don't try to save me. Save the two children that I have hidden. Let me go. I am going to a 'wedding'." What she meant by "wedding" is that she was going to a happy place.

They had an Armenian neighbour living in the house next door called Santucht. She also resisted not wanting to adopt the Turkish culture even to save herself. In fear for her life, she also hid under the floor of her house just as Nouritsa was hidden. The water system was such that fresh water would flow along open channels from under one house to the next. That was how water was distributed. An opening in the floor would enable access. Unfortunately, there was not enough space under the floor for an adult. Nouritsa, being physically small, was completely under the floor but Santucht was unable to get completely under. Her feet were sticking out above the ground. Nouritsa could see Santucht from across the underground space as their two houses were close to each other. After murdering the women they had rounded up, the killers went searching for any more that they missed. They spotted Santucht's feet sticking out from the under floor space: "Get out, get out, get out!" they shouted.

Nouritsa saw them dragging her out. She realised that once Santucht was out, they would likely look for others hiding in the space. They would find her. Even though she was much further away, she was sure they would find her. There happened to be some hay near her so she crept over and hid under it.

My grandmother was now gone but Nazely returned to the house. She returned as they pulled Santucht out from the under floor space. Santucht ran to Nazely and clung to her desperately. Through fear she had lost her voice and all she could do was cling to Nazely in desperation. Nazely's heart was broken in pieces seeing this and having just seen her mother go to her death. When it was safe, Nazely came to the place where Nouritsa was hiding from above. She had heard Nouritsa moving about and knew she was hiding below. She said from above: "Nouritsa, Nouritsa. That was such a great idea you had to move away from Santucht. How did you think of that! Stay there and do not move. I am here. Don't be frightened."

The frenzied attack on the Armenian women and children then subsided. The Turkish thugs that carried out the instructions from the authorities were able, at that time, to commit all sorts of atrocities. The children were at risk of being murdered too and so had to be hidden. Now the attack was over, the children could be taken in by the Turkish families.

New Turkish Family

Nazely was now my mother Nouritsa's and Melkon's guardian. However, Ahmed wanted to relocate to his old village and take only Melkon with them. He did not want Nouritsa, a girl. Ahmed had a sister who lived in yet another village. She was married but did not have a child so they agreed to take Nouritsa to her and she would become their daughter. They put some supplies for Nouritsa on a donkey and sent her to his sister in the other village. Melkon went with Nazely and Ahmed to his village. That is the point my mother was separated from her brother and sister. From that point, she did not see them for 40 years. 40 years later, however, she managed to track Melkon down with great difficulty and they were reunited. Nouritsa, who would have been about 6 or 7 years old at this time, remembers being put on a donkey and being taken to her new Turkish family. She felt the sorrow of not seeing her old village or relatives anymore. She stayed at the Turkish village with her new Turkish mother and father for quite a long time. She does not know exactly but thinks it may have been for 4 years. Her Turkish mother was called Anna and her Turkish father was called Mehmet. They changed my mother's name from the Armenian name "Nouritsa" to the Turkish name "Elmayee". She spoke with them in Turkish. That is all she knew anyway, she did not know Armenian at that point in time. They were also farmers. They would go to work in the fields in the mornings. Nouritsa's job was to help them by taking a boiled egg or some yoghurt at a certain time to their place of work. She would put the items they wanted on a donkey and head off to the field at the designated time.

Anna looked after Nouritsa well but she had a temper. If Nouritsa did something wrong, Anna would get very angry and discipline her as any mother would. Nevertheless, due to the trauma that Nouritsa suffered, Anna's normal behaviour would trigger great fear in my mother and she would run out of the house. Mehmet would sometimes intervene and remind Anna that Nouritsa was like a little bird that had found a branch and needed to feel safe. He was very kind and went out of his way to be extra kind to her due to her traumatic past. This overreaction by Nouritsa, however, worried Anna. She went to speak with her Armenian neighbour, who was married to a Turkish man. Anna thought maybe she could get her, as an Armenian, to talk to Nouritsa.   Anna said to the Armenian neighbour: "I have enemies. I have friends. I do not want them to know my personal business. When I try to discipline Elmayee, she raises her hands and runs out of the house in a crazed manner. Can you please talk to her? She may listen to you, as you are Armenian. If you can, convince her at least not to run out of the house when she gets frightened. Tell her if she needs to run away from me at least stay in the house. But let her know that I love her and am only doing my job as a mother by disciplining her."

The Armenian neighbour then went to talk to Nouritsa. "Why do you run out of the house when she yells at you? She is a good woman and is doing what is best for you under the circumstances."

Nouritsa explained: "I am frightened she will beat me or kill me. That is why I run away."

The Armenian neighbour calmed Nouritsa: "Don't run away like that. They are looking after you well. There is no need for that."   Then she did a superstitious good luck ceremony by making two fists and bashing them together saying, "They can do nothing to harm you!" This would make Nouritsa feel better and she adapted well to her new life. Soon her life was turned upside down yet again.

Returned to Armenian Community

The political situation was now changing. The war was over and the Ottoman Empire was being carved up by the European powers. As such, the Armenian community was able to organise a nationwide search for the missing Armenians. Their intention was to rebuild the Armenian nation. Any Armenian still alive would be collected and reunited with their property and family wherever possible. Whatever they had: a cow, a goat, a daughter, a wife - they were collecting them. If an Armenian was married or was now someone's child, the new authorities would come and collect them. This must have been around 1920. The Armenian neighbour found Nouritsa and said to her: "You are being rescued. Please rescue me as well." Nouritsa did not understand what she meant. Due to the fear of being found to want to return to the Armenians, the neighbour did not want to contact the Armenians herself but wanted Nouritsa to inform them about her. That way, they would come and return her to her Armenian community.

At this time, Anna said to Nouritsa: "Elmayee, do you understand they are collecting Armenians now? When the war ended we started living under new authorities. This order has been issued by the new authorities. If someone knocks on the door don't open the door. Otherwise they might take you away from us."

Nouritsa replied: "Ok. If someone knocks on the door, I will not open it".

One day, while Nouritsa was home alone, there was a knock at the door. Nouritsa had not forgotten about the instruction not to open the door but ran and opened the door anyway. At the door were three men. One of them asked: "Is there an Armenian girl living here?"

Fear suddenly gripped Nouritsa. Memories from her past came rushing back. She thought the Turkish thugs had come again to take her away to be slaughtered. Therefore, she panicked and slammed the door in their faces while shouting: "I have rejected the false Christian faith and have now accepted the true Islamic faith!"

When Anna came home later in the evening. Nouritsa explained what happened: "Mother, please forgive me. You told me many times not to open the door but I made a mistake and opened it."

Anna, concerned, said: "Oh my dear Elmayee, tell me exactly what happened."

Nouritsa told her: "Three men came to the house and said 'There is an infidel girl here and we have come to take her away.'"

Anna asked: "And what did you say to them?"

Nouritsa replied: "I slammed the door in their faces."

Anna said: "Well done. You did well."

On that, she sat Nouritsa on her lap and hugged her and kissed her. Later that night, when Mehmet came home, Anna said: "Elmayee has something important to tell you."

Mehmet was a very good and decent man. He was always concerned for Nouritsa, doing everything he could to give her a good life. He was well aware of the trauma she had suffered and went out of his way to lift her spirits.

Nouritsa told him: "Three men knocked on the door looking for an infidel girl. I told them I renounced the false faith and accepted the true faith. There is no Armenian girl here."

On that, Mehmet said: "Oh dear. You are no longer hidden from them. They have found you. We have to turn you over to them with our own hands. The authorities have issued such an order that we must hand you over ourselves. You have been discovered and so you are no longer able to stay with us. I'm so sorry."

Nouritsa was confused and frightened. She hugged his neck and cried: "Why father? Who are you going to hand me over to? I don't want to go."

Mehmet said: "We have to hand you over. The order is from a high authority. We will be punished if we don't."

Nouritsa asked: "Who will you give me to? What will you do?"

Mehmet said: "I will hand you over to the Armenian Millet. They are collecting you".

Nouritsa asked: "Father, what does Armenian Millet mean?"

Mehmet explained: "My daughter, the Armenian people have their Armenian Millet. The Greek people have their Greek Millet. We, Turkish people, have our Turkish Millet. There are many Millets in our country where each group of people live. The authorities govern all the Millets."

They took Nouritsa to the mayor's house where his wife tended to her. Nouritsa protested at being taken away from her Turkish family but she had no choice in the matter. She spent the night there. The following day they took her to a man who was from her home village of Gurden. He was a relative of my grandmother. The man said to Nouritsa: "My child, why did you object to being taken away from the Turkish family? Don't you want to be reunited with your Armenian people."

Nouritsa replied: "I don't know where you will take me. And I don't know what you mean by being reunited with my Armenian people."

Attempt to Reunite With Uncle

Nouritsa's eldest brother, Mihran, was a soldier away on duty when the troubles began. He had survived and was now living in the city of Adana. Adana was a major city in the southern region of Cilicia, which today is part of modern day Turkey. After the fall of the Ottoman Empire at the end of the First World War, the French had been assigned the mandate for governing Cilicia. As part of the mandate they were repatriating Armenians to Adana, though later in 1921 they pulled out and handed it over to the new Turkish government of Mustapha Kemal Attaturk. Mihran did not want to go back to his village of Gurden but was looking for any family he had left there. He instructed his friend to go to Gurden and bring back any relatives he could find that were still alive. The friend went to Gurden and searched all over. He found Mihran's wife and told her about Mihran, that he was alive and wants her and the children to go to him in Adana. She refused to go, however. She explained that things had changed as she was now married to a Turkish man and had a child with him also. She had already gone through hell and things had now settled down for her. She was now used to the current life and the new family. Mihran's friend then went and found Nouritsa's sister Nazely who said the same thing. She also had children with her Turkish husband. She had a new life and so did not go either.

Although Nouritsa was taken back to her home village of Gurden, Mihran's friend did not manage to track her down. The man temporarily responsible for Nouritsa, however, did find out she had family. He said: "I have discovered that you have an uncle from your father's side in Gessaria. I will send you to him. If he accepts to keep you with him, you will stay there. If not, there is an orphanage there and he can place you in their care until another relative can be found for you."

The man then handed Nouritsa over to an Armenian woman and her son. They lived in Gurden but would regularly go to Gessaria and sell their wares. The man arranged for them to take Nouritsa with them and deliver her to my uncle. On the journey to Gessaria with Nouritsa was another orphaned girl like her. The poor girl had suffered even more than Nouritsa. She was also recently retrieved from her Turkish guardians. However, these guardians, unlike Nouritsa's, treated her very badly. They would pull her hair and force her to carry hot bricks as punishment. They would put her food on the floor and make her eat like a cat licking from the floor. They all set off. A day and a half later, they still had not reached Gessaria. Their feet were burning as they walked without shoes. They had no shoes. Nouritsa remembers being hungry all the time. The woman had given them something to eat once but that was it. The hunger was terrible.

One night they came across a father and son who had set up camp for the night. They were also merchants transporting their goods via a horse drawn cart. Nouritsa remembers seeing their lanterns in the dark as the woman transporting her also set up camp nearby. Soon everyone went to sleep. The other orphaned girl then lay down next to Nouritsa and woke her up saying "Elma, Elma, Elma". They still called her "Elma" at that time and not "Nourtisa".

"What is it, girl?" said Nouritsa.

"Do you want some bread? Are you hungry? Do you want to eat?" said the other girl in Turkish.

The orphan girl had somehow managed to sneak into the other merchant's cart and steal a large piece of basterma and a loaf of bread from them. Basterma is air-dried, seasoned cured beef that is common in the region. She gave Nouritsa some Basterma and bread and they ate while lying there. The father and son that were with them were also lying there resting. They were not asleep but did not notice Nouritsa eating. Nouritsa and the other girl ate until they were full. There was some left over. The other girl said: "We should save that and eat it later."

Nouritsa then said: "But it's getting light. If they see the piece with us what will we do? Why don't we eat the remaining piece as well? At least that way there would be nothing to find."

The other girl agreed and so they both ate the remaining piece as well. They ate like cats, eating while they lay down. They were no longer hungry.

In the morning when they got up, they were frightened. They feared the others would work out that they had stolen and eaten the Basterma. Maybe they would smell it on their breath. However, they either did not notice or did not care. No one said anything. They just loaded the donkeys and continued on their way. Nouritsa and the girl were so relieved and their stomachs were full.

They continued walking to Gessaria. When they eventually reached there, the woman said to Nouritsa: "Listen to me child, I don't want your uncle to be angry with me. He may resent me for bringing you to him as you may be a burden to him. If he does not, perhaps his wife will. The people from Gessaria are a bit selfish like that. He may push you back onto me and I cannot look after you. No, I will not come with you but I will tell you where to go. You will need to go by yourself."

She explained the route to Nouritsa and off she went. She gave directions to the other girl too and that is where Nouritsa saw the last of her. Nouritsa reached the place she was directed to. There, she asked some people if they knew the "Basterma Maker" Hagop Ayvazyan. The people pointed to a house on a hill. One of them went ahead and called to Hagop's wife: "Haji-Lemon! Haji-Lemon! There is someone looking for you."

Although Hagop and Lemon were Nouritsa's uncle and aunt, they did not know each other. Nouritsa arrived as Lemon was busy peeling garlic on the roof with some others. She was working preparing the garlic, which is one of the main ingredients for making Basterma. On hearing the call for her name, Lemon left the others and came down. She took Nouritsa inside and asked her to sit down. She gave her a big piece of pastry, which Nouritsa gobbled up as she was so hungry.

"What happened to your father? What happened to your mother?" Lemon asked and started talking and making enquiries about her. Lemon's daughter was also there. However, Nouritsa was very tired from the long two-day journey. Her feet were in pain and she had no desire for a long chat. Lemon took a dislike to Nouritsa and all the changes her permanent presence would mean for them. That evening Nouritsa's uncle, Hagop, came home. As soon as he came, Lemon said: "You stay here with your uncle, my daughter and I will find somewhere else to stay." On this, they left the house. Lemon made it perfectly clear to her husband she will not live under the same roof as his niece.

"I am Nouritsa, the daughter of your brother Garabed." Nouritsa said to him. She then explained all that happened to her and how she came to be there. How her father and older brothers were murdered, how her sister married a Turk so they do not kill her, how her mother refused to do the same and was killed along with her grandfather. She explained how she was left with a Turkish family for a number of years. How she was then taken away from them by Armenians who gave her to a woman to deliver her here. Hagop wanted to find out more and managed to track down the woman that brought her from Gurden. He discussed things with the woman. He discussed how she came across Nouritsa, who instructed her, how she brought her there etc. The woman explained everything to him. Hagop could see Nouritsa was exhausted and so showed her to her bed. Nouritsa lay down and slept. When she woke up in the morning, she turned to her side and stayed there awake. My poor mother must have been about 10 years old at the time and had been through so much already. Yet she still faced an uncertain future. She knew her uncle might not be able to take her in. Hagop was washing his face there. He saw Nouritsa awake and said to her: "What can I do my dear. You saw my wife leave the house when I came home. What can I do?"

Hagop was full of emotion. He was torn between his duty to his dead brother and his duty to raise his own family without the additional burden of another mouth to feed. His wife's refusal to accept her made it even more difficult as he also had to choose between my mother and his wife. He continued sadly: "You are my brother's child but I cannot keep you here with me. I must take you to the orphanage where they can look after you properly."

He could see Nouritsa was in tears at his rejection but he felt he had no choice. He continued: "I'll take you to the orphanage and you will sit at the front gate. When the headmaster comes, say to him that you are an orphan. If you say that, they will take you in. Do not tell them you have an uncle. If you say that, they will not take you." He then took my mother to the orphanage. That was the last she heard from her uncle, Hagop Ayvazyan.

Placed in Orphanage

Nouritsa sat helpless and rejected at the gates to the orphanage. She must have been about 10 years old at the time and had been through so much already. After a time, a woman came out to her. She was her sister-in-law, her murdered brother Alexan's wife. She had survived too and found a job making bread in the orphanage. She tried to take Nouritsa inside, so she would be out of the hot sun but the guard at the gate did not allow this. The guard insisted they wait for the headmaster. He said: "When the headmaster arrives, he will decide if you can come in." So Nouritsa waited there with her sister-in-law. When the headmaster eventually arrived, he spoke to Nouritsa and then took her in. Nouritsa's sister in law had her son working at the orphanage also. So at least she had some family there. She spent the next few weeks there. The orphanage were collecting Armenian orphans but they had very little food or resources to handle the numbers they had. They were struggling to look after the orphans. They announced that anyone with a relative in a known location could be sent there. They just had to let the orphanage know and they would arrange the transport.

Nouritsa had heard about her brother Mihran being in Adana. This sparked new hope in her and she had to cling to it. She told the orphanage that she would like to go to Adana where her brother was. This upset Nouritsa's sister-in-law when she found out: "Why did you do that! You don't know where he is or anything about it why did you agree? I could have taken you to him later." She went and asked the leaders to cancel Nouritsa's registration. However, they did not accept her request. They said as she has a brother in Adana she must go there.

The orphanage hired six horse-drawn carts. On those, Nouritsa along with a number of other orphans, set off on the long journey to Adana. The journey was expected to take several days through the cold winter. Nouritsa remembers snow was falling at the time they set off. Due to the lack of resources, the orphans set off with no shoes on their feet and inappropriate thin summer clothing. This was not suitable for the long journey but they had no option. They sat in the cart and huddled together as they were very cold. On the way, they stopped and slept in barns and whatever shelter they could find. Sometimes it would rain at night and they would be glad to be in the shelter. Although there were no fires, the animal waste in the barns gave off some heat which kept them a little warm. The cart drivers were Turkish and would drive in a convoy. The drivers, however, would not be very close to each other. At one point the driver of my mother's cart saw his horses were tired and struggling to pull uphill. He exclaimed: "Everybody out of the cart! My horses are exhausted and are not pulling you up that hill. Instead of my horses dying – you die, you infidels!"

He forced Nouritsa and the other orphans off the cart and left. The children walked through the snow in the direction of the other carts up ahead. Nouritsa grew weary and, overcome with exhaustion, collapsed. She lay on the ground as the other children walked on, leaving her behind. Nouritsa's unconscious body was slowly being covered by the falling snow. An Armenian family, in a cart of their own, was part of the convoy going to Adana. As they drove along, they spotted my mother on the ground in the snow. The head of the family collected her and put her in their cart. They covered her with a blanket and warmed her body. Nouritsa regained consciousness but was still very weak. On noticing this, the man said: "You need to stay awake or you will die." They encouraged Nouritsa to stay awake. They then fed her.

The next day they managed to get Nouritsa to the convoy that had gone on ahead. Now back onto the cart for the orphans, they stopped at a place called: "Benemedic". It was a French controlled region with many soldiers stationed there. As the carts drove through, Nouritsa could hear the soldiers exclaim: "The orphans are coming! The orphans are coming!" The French soldiers stood and saluted them as the orphans arrived. They then fed them as they spent one night there. Nouritsa remembers eating potatoes, meat and rice. The following day a train pulled up to the local station. The soldiers put the orphans on the train and sent them off to Adana. Nouritsa suffered a lot on the train. There was no water and conditions were very cramped in the carriage. The train made a short stop. Nouritsa remembers they were told to get off for a short time and that it was dark when this happened. The organisers offered the orphans something to drink. Nouritsa remembers drinking but also, as it was dark, worried about whether the drink was contaminated with insects. She drank anyway as she was so thirsty. After their drink, the orphans rested there for a little while. Then the train whistle blew so they all got back on the train. Another orphan girl grabbed Nouritsa by the hand and pulled her on-board. The train continued until it finally arrived at the Adana train station. There, the orphans got off and were lead a long way through the vineyards, thorns and vegetation to reach the orphanage. As they did so, they were soaked through due to the heavy rain. That is where they spent the night.

In the morning, the sun shone and the orphans lined up to dry under its heat. The orphanage they reached was actually the French Army barracks in Adana. The French organisers came and separated the orphans into ones who had relatives and ones that did not. Nobody came for my mother so they took her to the nearby school. They looked after Nouritsa and the other orphans at the school for about a year. There were Armenians working at the school but it was managed by the French. Nouritsa thought her brother Mihran would come. He did not come and she never heard from him.

Escape to Cyprus

The year must have been 1921 because Nouritsa remembers the people around her exclaiming with fear: "Kemal is coming!" Around that time, Mustapha Kemal Attaturk managed to rally the Turkish nation that had been beaten in the First World War. He managed to strengthen the Turkish nation and win back territory it had lost. As such, Adana was in his sights and he was not far away. Though Adana was under French control, the French were spread very thinly in the Cilicia mandate and had decided to leave. The French leaders said they were going to leave and told the Armenian leaders of the orphanage to decide what they wanted to do. As they would be losing French protection, the Armenian leaders thought it best to transport the orphans from Adana to Mersin. In Mersin there was a port and it would be possible to escape by boat from there if necessary. In Adana there was no chance of getting away if Kemal came there. For this reason they left Adana. It was not just the orphans but also the local population. Nouritsa was taken to Mersin and she stayed there for a time. However, it soon became clear that Kemal was coming to take Mersin too. The orphanage managers were desperate to save the orphans and so placed an advertisement on the orphanage gate: "If you can rescue an Armenian orphan, please come inside and register." A man with a family escaping from Gessaria came to Nouritsa. He did not have a girl. He had three young boys, the oldest being 8 years old. He took Nouritsa with them and eventually brought her to Cyprus. Unfortunately, he was unable to find a job in Cyprus and was not doing so well financially. For this reason, he was forced to leave Nouritsa with another family as he emigrated to Beirut, Lebanon. He left my mother, Nouritsa, with the Sultanian family in Nicosia. She stayed at the Sultanian house for five years until she met and married Hovhannes Kiremidjian, my father. After experiencing several years of life-changing events where she lost her family and was sent from place to place, Nouritsa finally had someone that could provide her with stability in her life. Though there were more hardships to come, Hovhannes was now with her.

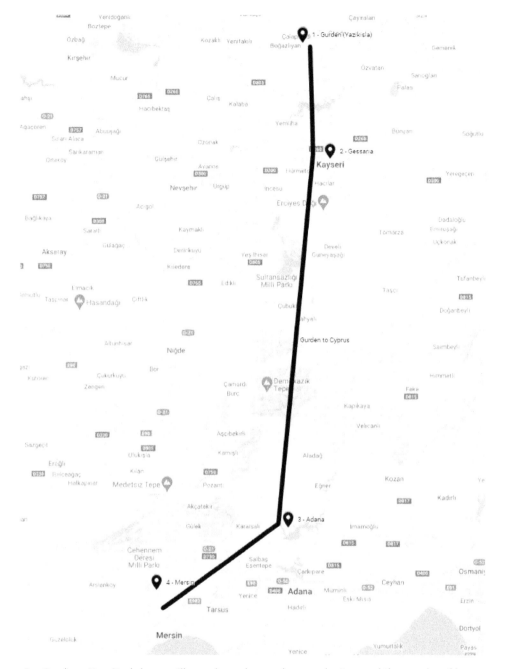

1. Gurden. Nouritsa's home village where she was born and witnessed the murder of her family in 1915.
2. Gessaria. Nouritsa was rejected by her uncle Hagop and sent to an orphanage.
3. Adana. Nouritsa was transferred to another orphanage thinking incorrectly that her brother Mihran would come to collect her.
4. Mersin. The orphanage at Adana escaped the advance of Ataturk by getting to the port of Mersin. From here Nouritsa caught a ship to Cyprus.

Summary Thoughts

Every night before my bedtime, my mother would tell me snippets of this story. Sometimes it would be about how she was feeling when she fell in the snow expecting to die. Sometimes it was about the anxiety she would experience living with her kind Turkish parents for a few years. My mother would break out in emotion and tears and we would hug tightly for comfort. She would say I am now her mother and her father and her family. These stories caused me nightmares and affected me deeply but I do not regret her telling me any of it.

My Father's Story

The story that follows is my father's account of the horror he went through as an adolescent. It covers the time from his early childhood until he escaped to Cyprus but also goes on to cover his early life and economic struggles in Cyprus. Robert recorded him on video as he told this story in Armenian. I then translated the words he spoke into English. Here, you will see the transcript transformed into a more easy to follow narration that includes things he had told me over the years. My father's earliest memories were also very traumatic. Even though he did not witness the worst of the Armenian Genocide, it was still horrific and his life at the time was turned upside down.

Hovhannes Kiremidjian telling his story in 1992

He was born in 1903 in a village south of Istanbul called Soloz. As the First World War started, he was forced to leave Soloz for another Ottoman village for "safety". He and the family suffered a lot during this time away from Soloz including attempts on their lives. After 1918 when the war ended, he and his family were able to go back to Soloz. They got on with their lives under Greek and British rule which meant no more fear of persecution for being Armenian. Then, due to Ataturk's advances in 1923, he was forced to leave his home again. Escaping for his life he made his way to the port of Mudanya where he escaped to Greece and then to Cyprus. His early years in Cyprus was a huge struggle due to financial uncertainty but he managed to get through it all and give his children the hope of a better life.

Early Soloz Life

Hovhannes, my father, was raised by his parents: Toros and Flora. He had three brothers and one sister. His oldest brother, Mirijan, went into the Ottoman army as a soldier at the start of the First World War and never returned. The next eldest was Zareh, then his sister Chrissy. Hovhannes was the fourth child. After him was his youngest brother, Krikor. His father, Toros, was a choirmaster that had studied at the famous Armash Monastery. Toros was the eldest and had four younger brothers: Melkon, then Nishan and finally there was Hagop. Hagop and Nishan were builders. Melkon was a farmer.

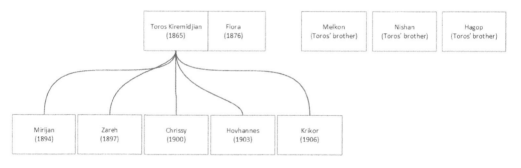

Hovhannes' family tree

Toros was a music teacher. Just prior to the Genocide of 1915, their village was very prosperous. There was a police station, a hotel, a tailor, a carpenter as well as several factories. The family business was in silk and olive oil production. The olive oil was very plentiful. They had everything, even a doctor and a pharmacy. That is the kind of village, Soloz, was. Every week there would be a market. The Turkish villagers from the region would bring yoghurt and butter to a local market called "Alank".   There, the Turkish villagers would come and trade with the Armenian villagers. The Armenians could find all they needed there. The village had a church called "Church of the Archangel". There were two schools: one school for boys and one for girls. The schools did not allow the boys and girls to interact with each other. The boys and girls had lessons and played separately. The school's three storey buildings were built next to each other as was common at the time. As a choirmaster, my grandfather would teach Hovhannes and his siblings to sing and read the Bible. Hovhannes remembers being taught to sing in an alternating pattern i.e. Hovhannes would sing, then his partner would sing and then he would sing again. The church recognised he had a good singing voice and so selected him to sing in the church and gave him a role as a deacon. There was also some trouble from time to time. They would have trouble with the people of the neighbouring Turkish village of "Tutluja". My father recalls those people being particularly nasty people. They were fanatic Turks in his eyes. When they ventured into the nearby hills on the outskirts of both villages, they would take pot shots at each other with their rifles. Either the Turks would shoot at my father's villagers or my father's villagers would shoot at them. Their village of Soloz had yet another village nearby that was referred to as the "Turkish Soloz" village. He remembers that the olive groves of the two villages were mixed. The Turkish Soloz people would come into my father's olive groves and my father would go to theirs. Hovhannes did not fear them even though as Armenians they were a minority in the Ottoman Empire.

Deportations

On 15 August 1914, the authorities deported Hovhannes's family from their village of Soloz along with the other Armenians. This was mandatory and explained as for their protection due to the First World War. They packed as much of their belongings as they could carry and departed. The authorities were providing instructions and guides to ensure Hovhannes's family and many other Armenians reached their destinations. The first destination was Mechijeh Train Station, which they reached on foot. From there, they got a train to Eskisheyir. From there, they then caught another train to Konia. They stayed at Konia for about three weeks. When they got there, they went to the Konia fields with the other Western Armenian refugees. There were around a hundred thousand refugees like them brought to Konia. While there, Hovhannes noticed many of the refugees were getting sick. Typhus was spreading there due to the bad sanitary conditions and he saw tens of people dying every day around them.

As Hovhannes's brother, Mirijan, was a soldier and some of his uncles had been soldiers, they were classified as "families of soldiers". As such, they were treated differently to other families. They had a few more privileges. These privileges included things like being considered more trust-worthy in the case of a legal disagreement. It also meant they had more influence on the authorities and so their request to be moved out from the disease-infested Konia was granted. They were moved on to Beysheyir by foot. This meant a few days of walking while carrying their belongings. It was hard. They walked and walked. On the first day when it got dark, they had to rest and so spent the night at a village along the way. They found accommodation and prepared to sleep there as a family. There were about twenty of them altogether. All Hovhannes's extended family was with them: from the very young to the very old. This included grandfather Toros' brothers and their families.

Inside they thought they were safe and so were preparing to sleep but some young Turkish thugs began to trouble them. From outside the room they threatened: "Infidels, we will kill the older ones and steal the little ones from you!" They tried to gain entry from the flimsy thin door. In fact, the door was in such poor condition Hovhannes thought it could easily fall off the hinges with a little shove. He says they had a miraculous escape and that it was due to his mother, Flora, going down on her knees with the children and praying to God for help. Somehow, the Turks did not manage to get through the door. Flora got them all to shout and make a commotion to draw as much attention to what was going on to outsiders in the hope this would make the thugs think twice about what they were doing. The thugs did not manage to open the door. However, they continued with their threats: "Give us money and we will leave you alone."

Flora responded: "I don't know if we have any money. If I can find some coins among the children I will give them to you." On that, she collected five pennies and offered it to them through a window. They took the pennies and left them in peace for the rest of the night. After the ordeal, the family slept.

The next morning, at dawn, they set off on the road again. There were other Armenian families with them and the authorities were still directing them to their destinations. They knew where their immediate next destination was but not their final destination. With worn out shoes and worn out clothes they continued on the road to Beysheyir. Their feet began to crack and bleed from the walking. They continued through the pain. There were no proper roads back then and, at times, they had to ask for directions along the way. They suffered a lot on that exhausting journey but eventually saw Beysheyir in the distance. The moment they got there, a man called Hovhannes met them and gave them a freshly baked loaf of bread. The hungry family ate it immediately. Hovhannes recalls that it was so delicious that even until the day of our video interview the taste of it was still in his mouth. This man Hovhannes, who had the same name as my father, was in Beysheyir with his friend Gourlou. They had arrived not too long ago from Istanbul. They were popular among the Armenian refugees who referred to them as "effendi", a Turkish term used to show respect. In Istanbul, they had both worked in a German company and knew many influential people. They had managed to use their influence and get on good terms with the governor of Beysheyir. In this way, they were able to help the Armenians to a certain extent.

Not long later, the Turkish authorities in Beysheyir initiated "Sevkiat", meaning the action of sending the Armenians and other minorities out to another place. Again they were moved, this time to one of the villages outside Beysheyir. They were transported along with about 60 to 100 families. By chance, Hovhannes's family were moved to a village called "Homar" which was a flat and dry place. They stayed there with tens of other Armenian families. After a few days they noticed, however, that many of the people there were dying of Typhus due to the conditions they were living in. Due to the risk of catching the disease and dying, my father's family applied to be moved to another village. This right to request such relocation was part of their privileges as a family of a soldier. Their request to be moved was granted and they were moved to Karatay village.

Karatay Village

So, after moving around from place to place, they finally had some stability in Karatay village. They stayed there, working for their living, for the next 3 years until the 1918 ceasefire and the end of the First World War. During this time in Karatay village, my father explained that a lot happened but only elaborated on how his brother killed a Turkish man in self-defence and how he was almost murdered in revenge. Zareh, his older brother, had found a job working at the local mill. One night, while he was working alone, several thugs went to him looking to cause trouble. It was common for such thugs to target Armenian minorities. The Turkish thugs took wheat to him and demanded: "Mill our wheat. We need flour." Zareh could sense there was going to be trouble but wanted to do his best to avoid it. As he was already part way through milling someone else's wheat, he responded: "OK, but please let me complete the process of milling this wheat already in the mill and then I can start on yours. This wheat belongs to another customer and I cannot remove it without seeing the process through."

The thugs, however, were insistent that he mill their wheat immediately: "I don't care about that. You will mill my wheat right now!"

Seeing they were not being reasonable and sensing trouble, Zareh responded: "OK, please be patient and I will go and stop the water so the mill stops and the stone grinder stops." He said this to them but that was not his intention. He knew they had come to kill him and so he wanted to get a weapon. Zareh's boss, Karamustapha the owner of the mill, had left him a pistol and some bullets. As he left the thugs on the pretence to stop the water, he took the pistol and ran out of the mill taking cover behind a rock. They saw him run out and began shooting at him. The thugs were inside the mill and he was outside. After many exchanged shots, Zareh was down to his last few bullets. One of the thugs ran out of the door towards him. Zareh took aim at his chest and shot him. He fell to the floor dead and the others ran away. Zareh then realised he would be hunted down for his actions even though it was self-defence. They would either put him in prison or kill him. Zareh went to his sister Chrissy: "Sister, give me a loaf of bread. I need to go away."

Chrissy said: "Zareh, what are you going to do?"

Zareh replied: "I will leave the village and live out in the wild. Otherwise these thugs will come for me again." He took the bread and ran off to the hills and joined a group of bandits. There were about 20 of them. They were mostly Turkish but some were Armenian. These men survived by robbing people on the roads and living out in the wild.

One day while they were living like this, they found themselves on the outskirts of Konia. Zareh saw some soldiers on horses coming towards them and realised they were coming to arrest them. As the forest was not far, they ran and took cover in the forest. The soldiers caught up with them and a shootout started. After a long battle, the five Armenian bandits split away from the other Turkish bandits. As they did this, they also managed to get away from the soldiers. They survived in that smaller Armenian group until the 1918 ceasefire. After the end of the war, Zareh returned to Soloz. He returned via Reyal and then Konia along with lots of Armenians making their way back to their homes.

At the time when uncle Zareh killed his attacker, it would have been early 1918 and Hovhannes was 15 years old. Hovhannes was working as a labourer on a Turkish man's farm. There was uproar in the fields among the Turkish community. A friend of the dead man went to the field where Hovhannes was hard at work. It was about noon. He approached Hovhannes with a sword and said: "Infidel I am going to kill you!"

Hovhannes, stunned, managed to ask: "Why?"

He responded: "Our Turk was killed by an infidel and so I will kill you to get vengeance!"

When he said that, Hovhannes ran but the Turk gave chase waving his sword. Fortunately, he could not catch Hovhannes who was strong and could run fast. Hovhannes reached the animal shelter where his employer was expecting him later in the day. He did not stop to see his employer, however, and continued running. When his attacker also reached the animal shelter, my father's Turkish employer confronted him: "What do you want with him?" He demanded.

The attacker said: "An infidel killed our Turk and I am seeking revenge. I will kill that Armenian man!"

My father's Turkish employer said: "Who killed your friend? It was not this man. Find the killer and kill him. Not this man. This man is a useful worker to me!"

Hovhannes was thus under the protection of his Turkish employer for the duration of his stay in Karatay. In fact, Hovhannes would speak very highly of him and his wife. His wife would always feed and care for him very well, he would say.

Although a lot more clearly happened during their stay in Karatay village, my father did not expand on this during the interview. He simply explained they eventually went back to Soloz as the war ended.

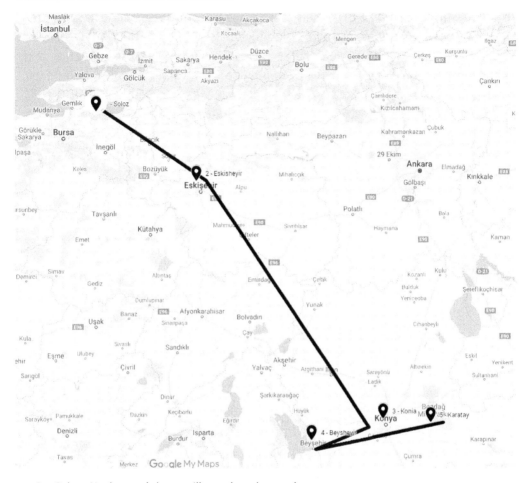

1. Soloz. Hovhannes's home village where he was born.
2. Eskisheyir. Hovhannes and his family stayed here initially as they we relocated from their home during the first world war.
3. Konia. The family then moved on to Konia for a few weeks where they witnessed the deaths of many Armenian refugees due to the sanitary conditions.
4. Beysheyir. At their own request to escape the poor conditions of Konia, the family was moved on to Beysheyir by foot. On route, they spent one night at an inn and were harassed by local thugs.
5. Karatay. After seeing further poor conditions where others were dying daily, the family moved on to Karatay village where they stayed for the next 3 years until 1918. This is where my uncle Zareh killed a man in self-defence.

The war ended in 1918 and the Ottoman Empire was falling apart. They lost control of much of the land they previously controlled as the western powers took over. The Ottomans still had control of some areas, however, and for a time that included Soloz. The new authorities instructed all refugees to go back to their home villages. The Tashnaks, an Armenian nationalist political group, gained in influence and started work to rebuild the Armenian communities. My father's family packed their things and left Karatay for Soloz. They went back via a convoluted route, initially taking a train from Konia to Constantinople (now called Istanbul). They spent a week there with their Armenian friends who put them up in an apartment and fed them. They found out that the Armenians in Constantinople were not deported like other Armenians from other villages. They then left Constantinople by boat to Gemleik and then from there on to Soloz village.

It was December when they finally returned home. Hovhannes remembers there being a metre or two layer of thick snow on the ground. They found a barren house with the doors and windows removed. Due to the cold, they immediately covered the openings with rugs and other material. In this way they managed to stay warm. When the snow melted, Hovhannes and some of the others went to do "Bashak". "Bashak" is the term given to the act of collecting the remaining olives that had fallen from the trees. They collected the fallen olives from the ground, put them in large containers and took them home. There, they separated out the good from the bad olives. They salted the good olives and crushed the bad, damaged olives to extract their oil. That year, the olives were plentiful and were sold at a high price due to the demand. They made a lot of money quite easily from their olives. However, the olive boom was not sufficient to offset the general economic downturn. The family had very little income and life was expensive. My grandfather, Toros, managed to get a job as a choirmaster but the pay was not much. A sack of flour at that time cost almost as much as he would earn in a week. He had six dependents to feed and was unable to support them on his salary alone. Hovhannes returned to school but only for one day because he needed to earn money to support his father. They were hungry at home and needed Hovhannes to contribute to the family finances. They found him a temporary job in a nearby Turkish village called Golcik. He went for 3 months but went willingly as he wanted to do something to improve the family's situation. On his return, Hovhannes did not go back to school but instead started work as a farmer on their land. He, along with the family, would plant beans, tomatoes, aubergines, sweetcorn and work the land to earn a living.

A year later, in 1919, the Greek army came to take the lands that had been allocated to them by the European powers. They came via the port at Smyrna (now called Izmir) and conquered all the way to Bursa. As news of them taking Bursa reached my father's village, they waited impatiently for the Greeks to come and conquer their village too. They wanted to be liberated from their Turkish rulers that had treated them as second-class citizens for so long and murdered many of their fellow Armenians living in other parts of the Ottoman lands. Genocide was major news at that time and the Armenians discussed it a lot within their communities. The Turkish authorities would prohibit the printing of such news in the local newspapers but my grandfather and others had influential Armenian contacts that would provide the news. They would receive news detailing what the Ottomans did and were still doing to the Armenians and this would help cement their alliance with the Greeks when they eventually came to Soloz. After about a six-month delay, the Greeks eventually came and conquered Gemleik and then Soloz. Then came the winter of 1919 and the cold weather. This resulted in the Greeks not wanting to continue their campaign to take the Turkish lands promised to them until the following summer. The following year when the weather improved, the Greeks continued on conquering Eskisheyir and then all the way up to Ankara. The Greeks stayed and governed the region from 1919 until 1921. During this time, under Greek rule, my father's family began to prosper economically. They reached a point where they were doing well and were earning a good living. Hovhannes went to work with his uncle Nishan as an apprentice builder. He would earn good money. His father and brothers were now all earning money and so all was good financially. The house was full of all the provisions they needed: wheat, barley, sweetcorn, beans – you name it they had plenty of it. It was also at this time that my Aunty Chrissy fell in love with a Greek soldier. She ended up marrying him and moving abroad to settle in British-controlled Cyprus. Unfortunately, this period of prosperity for my family did not last and they did not get the chance to enjoy it.

In 1921, the global geo-political game took a twist. France, Italy and Russia decided they no longer wanted Greece to take these lands. They feared the British, through their alliance with Greece, were becoming too powerful in the region. Therefore, they raised Mustafa Kemal Ataturk to power and reinvigorated the Turkish nation. As Mustafa Kemal got stronger, he hit back at Greece and slowly started taking back the lands Greece had conquered. The news then came that they were approaching Bursa. This meant Mustafa Kemal would soon overrun Soloz.

Escaping Ataturk

When the news came, my father's family had no choice but to escape Soloz. They knew the Turks did not look at them favourably even before the arrival of the Greeks. After the Greeks arrived and the Armenians supported them, it was clear the Turks would see the Armenians as the enemy and would not hold back to wipe them out. There was no way they could stay in Turkey let alone Soloz. Therefore, in 1921, they again left their village but this time with no intention of ever returning. The plan was to get to the nearby port of Gemleik and escape by boat. In preparation for their permanent departure, Hovhannes and his brothers and cousins travelled for several days transporting their provisions to Gemleik intending to make use of them there. They made multiple journeys loading their cart at home and then emptying at a store in Gemleik. Unfortunately, it turned out that their efforts were in vain, as they could not use their provisions in Gemleik and they had to abandon them there. Not only that, they also had to leave much of their provisions in their house, as it was too much to carry.

Hovhannes, grandfather Toros, uncle Zareh and my father's cousin Ohanik left Soloz separately from the rest of the extended family as they were busy sorting out the last of the cartload of provisions. The plan was to meet up on the road to the port of Gemleik. It was an emotional time for Hovhannes, who left the house for the last time and started on the journey. He left his home, his farm and even the new calf that was recently born. They had not gone far when, from Lower Soloz, they encountered Greek soldiers. These soldiers had just come from the front and wanted Hovhannes to take them to Bursa. Hovhannes did not know the route and managed to convince them to leave them alone. Fortunately, the soldiers were a decent group and went on their way without any trouble. As they left, they told Hovhannes that if he came across any Greek soldiers on his journey, he should inform them the front is abandoned and that the Greeks were in retreat.

Hovhannes and the men continued on foot and approached a river just before reaching Tutluja. Hovhannes was supporting my elderly grandfather, as he was unable to walk easily. As they walked to the bridge to cross the river, soldiers on horseback intercepted them. Somehow, uncle Zareh and Ohanik managed to avoid being seen and hid nearby. Hovhannes and grandfather, however, were unable to react so quickly and were face to face with the soldiers. They asked, in Turkish. "Who are you?"

Hovhannes was frightened and feared for their lives. He did not know which side the soldiers were on. They could have been Greeks retreating like the previous ones they encountered or they could have been Turks ready to slaughter them. As he was not prepared, he decided it was best to speak the truth: "We are from Soloz." Said Hovhannes.

"You are Armenian?" Enquired the soldier.

"Yes" replied Hovhannes.

It turned out that they were also Armenian. They were armed auxiliary soldiers, not part of the main Greek army but on the same side. These soldiers, referred to as "Abazan", were not generally in uniform. Realising they were on the same side, they left them alone. Zareh and Ohanik then came out from their cover. They told

Hovhannes they were watching the soldiers' every move and if they moved to try to kill them, they would have come out and attacked them. Zareh had a hand grenade and Ohanik had a gun ready. After this scary ordeal, they continued their journey. A short while later they heard more soldiers on horseback approaching them in the dark. This time they all managed to jump to the side of the road to avoid being seen. As they did so, there were two paths available to them: one lead uphill and one lead downhill. Instead of taking the easier downhill path, they took the more difficult uphill one. They did this without thinking in their panicked state. My grandfather was old and struggling to walk up but the other younger men could easily make it. As they scaled the hill, they disturbed the loose soil and it fell downward creating a lot of noise. Hovhannes was worried they had given away their presence but the soldiers on horseback did not hear it. This was probably due to the noise of their horses as they galloped by.

Seeing the soldiers pass by without stopping, Hovhannes and the men continued. My father held my grandfather with one arm and an "Oghi" bottle in other. Oghi was a popular alcoholic drink similar to Ouzo. My father encouraged my grandfather to jog along so they travelled faster: "Come on dad, you can run, Come on dad you can run".

With the extra encouragement, my grandfather would pick up the pace. Afterwards, though, his energy would run low and he would struggle to continue at that speed. When Hovhannes could see he was struggling, he would give him a little Oghi and that would give him extra energy. They ran and ran for 20 minutes or so until they reached a campsite. From a distance, they could see people there but Hovhannes could not work out who they were. They knew they were near the village of Gurleh, an Armenian village, but they feared the people at the campsite could be Kemalist Turks. They approached slowly. It turned out it was a group of villagers from Soloz that they had caught up. The rest of my father's family was not among this group. The villagers were resting there for the night and planning to get to Gemleik the following morning. My father's group approached them and alerted them about the developments at the front: "The Greek soldiers have abandoned the front and are running for their lives. The Kemalists will be here very soon as there is no Greek army to hold them back! You need to get out of here. There is not much time. If they get here they will either kill you or take you prisoner!"

On that, the people wearily got up. Some were half-asleep but they packed their belongings back onto their donkeys and horses and continued. Hovhannes and the men went with them. To get to Gemleik, there was a mountainous route, which my grandmother and the other family members had taken and another non-mountainous route, which Hovhannes took. As Hovhannes reached Gemleik, he found there were Greek soldiers at the pass controlling entry. As they approached the soldiers, one of them shouted: "Ho!" instructing them to stop.

Hovhannes responded: "We are from Soloz. We have escaped from our home and looking to get on a ship and out of here." The soldiers let Hovhannes and the men pass into the town of Gemleik. They went through and met up with the rest of the family. It was daytime by now and they felt a little safer due to the Greek soldiers' presence. The immediate plan now was to go to the harbour and get on a boat out of there. Along with many others, my father's family started on the road to the coast where the harbour was. At this point, Hovhannes's lack of rest caught up with him. He was very tired as he was up all night getting to Gemleik. Additionally, the days prior, he was transporting their provisions from Soloz and so was continuously working for several days without much rest. Hovhannes desperately needed to rest and planned in his mind to lie down and sleep somewhere under a tree. My grandfather and grandmother were on a donkey heading towards the coast. Hovhannes called out to them and said: "I'll catch up don't worry, I just need to tie my shoe laces."

His intention was not to tie his shoes but to sleep and recover. He did not want to worry his parents about the fact that he was so tired and could not continue. He desperately needed to sleep. In the interview he used the phrase: "The sleep was pouring out from my eyes." So he slept. As he did so, he dreamt the Kemalists were capturing him as a prisoner. Immediately he woke up and saw he was by himself and in danger. He recalled the Turkish expression: "Dabana Kuvet", meaning "Power to your feet" and put all his strength into his legs and ran. He ran all the way to the coast, which was quite a distance and caught up with the family.

As the reunited family reached the coast, they were looking to get on a boat but they were too late. The Kemalists were at the outskirts of Gemleik and started hitting the harbour with cannon fire from the surrounding mountains. On seeing this, the boats left. The boats at the harbour were supposed to help evacuate the Greeks and any other refugees but, due to the cannons, they could not risk waiting at the shore for them to board. They would be sitting ducks and so they turned away and escaped themselves. My father's family were stranded at the port of Gemleik with the Turks surrounding them. There were around a hundred thousand Christian refugees with them. They had come from the east as the Turks advanced west. The Greeks, Armenians, Assyrians and other non-Turks were escaping and leaving their villages and homes. They all intended to escape by boat like Hovhannes's family but now faced the prospect of annihilation.

On seeing what had happened, the refugees were forced to abandon their plans of getting out from Gemleik by boat and instead head to Mudanya. Mudanya was another port town and to get there they had to walk for another day. So in desperation, the hundred thousand strong refugees, including Hovhannes's family, headed for Mudanya. The mass of refugees travelled together on the road to Mudanya. There was chaos as the panicked mass trampled over anyone that fell in their path. Many died in this manner and the ones escaping did not look at the ones that died underfoot. It was everyone for themselves as they looked to save their own families. From the distance, the Kemalists were firing at the mass of people and at the Greek soldiers who were also making a desperate attempt to escape. It was hell on earth.

Hovhannes's family were now all together and on the road to Mudanya. They continued well into the night at which point the road they were on became narrow. My grandmother and grandfather were on a horse drawn cart but not for much longer. The horses pulling the cart were hungry and thirsty and were not able to pull it any longer. Hovhannes hit them in a desperate attempt to get them moving but they could not. Therefore, my grandparents had to get off and walk. Hovhannes remembered that at one point on the road they were passing a house that was on fire. They could see the flames in the dark and feel the heat. This may have been caused by the Kemalists or possibly by the retreating Greek soldiers. The Greeks had adopted a scorched earth policy whereby they would burn down anything that would be of value to the advancing Kemalists. In any case, the building was about to collapse on them. God must have intervened as it collapsed just moments after they passed it. Hovhannes saw it collapse behind them.

They eventually made it to Mudanya but once there, the Kemalists held them captive for three days. What happened here is a little unclear to me as my father did not elaborate on this part of his story in any great detail. I suspect the Armenians, along with the Greek soldiers, somehow managed to make the overnight journey from Gemleik to Mudanya by holding off the Kemalist onslaught to a certain extent. The fact that the Kemalists held them captive in Mudanya must mean they eventually overpowered the Armenians and Greeks but they did this within the zone controlled by the foreign powers. The French military was present in Mudanya and so must have had influence over what the Kemalists did to their captives. I understand that the French arranged for the captives to be exiled and so the Kemalists could not simply annihilate them. The Armenians and Greeks were thus waiting to be put on boats and moved out.

During their three days of captivity in Mudanya, the Kemalists tormented the refugees. The Kemalist soldiers would come at night among the refugees and say things like: "Infidel, these shoes don't suit you" and would take them. "This dress is not good for you" and take them. They would take some of the girls away and do who knows what to them. After suffering this abuse for a couple of days, one of the

Armenian refugees approached the French General. This Armenian could speak English and French. He had previously been in the French army. He was called "Kojaghayents" and was a good man. He said to the French General: "You see what they are doing to us but you close your eyes! Look at my medals. I have fought in the French army. Do you not care for these people? They are suffering under these Turkish soldiers. The Turks are abusing us and you close your eyes. Is this right? You're Christian and the refugees are Christians."

The French General, moved by Kojaghayents' words, decided to act. He sent three French soldiers and an officer to the Kemalist leaders that were holding the refugees captive. The French Officer announced: "As of now, you will not abuse any of the Christians or Refugees you are holding. Any further abuse will not be tolerated and you will make enemies of the French."

The Armenian Patriarch of Constantinople had sent two boats to Mudanya to collect the Armenian refugees held there. Hovhannes saw two boats arrive at the harbour but had no information on where the boats were going to take them. As the refugees were told to board the boats, they carried their belongings and made their way on board. Hovhannes was carrying the large chest that my grandmother had given him to carry. He was helping the others get on board and so put the chest down on the platform temporarily. The family got on the boat and my grandmother reminded Hovhannes: "Hovhannes, don't forget the chest." Hovhannes went to get it but the people getting onto the boat caused the boat to tip one-way. The boat owner was shouting: "Go to the other side of the boat, the boat will sink." Nobody listened. Everyone was looking to save their soul they were not thinking about the boat sinking. As a result, the boat pulled away from the platform. Hovhannes was left on the platform separated from the family. Seeing this, my grandmother rushed to the boat worker and explained: "Please get my son Hovhannes who is still on the platform." She also gave him money. Hovhannes was still on the platform holding the large chest not knowing what to do. The boat came towards the platform and someone shouted from the boat: "Who is Hovhannes?"

Hovhannes responded with: "I am" and as he said the words he jumped on board. He threw the chest onto the boat and jumped on behind it. As he did so, one of his shoes fell into the water and so he was left with one shoe for the rest of the journey. They sat on the boat for a good long while. It became dark and they were waiting for the boat to depart. They were still fearful about Mustafa Kemal Ataturk. Maybe he would change his mind and not allow them to leave after all. This would mean defying the French but it was a possibility. The horn blew "brrrrr". It then blew a second time. As it blew for the third time, they made their cross sign because they knew on the third blowing the boat would depart. The boats engine noise was reassuring: "Shagh-shagh-shagh-shagh". They were now leaving Mudanya and their home by boat. They did not know where they were going, but they had survived a very difficult situation and they were glad.

The boat took them to Tekirdagh, which is 100km west of Istanbul and on the north coast of the Sea of Marmara. There they were taken off the boat and told that this was where they, and the many other Armenian refugees, can make their new home. The transportation of the Armenians was organised by various Armenian charity organisations. They had suffered a lot. They were refugees, having left everything behind. They were doing well back in Soloz due to their prospering business but now they had nothing. They had no money or any assets. What could they do to earn a living? My grandfather was choirmaster but there was no need for such skills. On the positive side, Hovhannes was in his late teens, strong and full of energy. In addition, my father's cousin Michael, was a natural businessman who could make money out of any situation. Michael led the young men in the family in a small business venture to make some money quickly. They would go to Tekirdagh fish market and buy salted fish. They would then go around the town finding customers to sell it at a profit. Another idea from Michael was to collect fire wood, break it to a standard size and sell it to the locals.

After a time, perhaps a few weeks, news came that the Kemalists were coming to conquer Tekirdagh too. My father's family and the other Armenian families now had to leave there too. At this time, the border between modern day Greece and Turkey was being determined and Hovhannes was caught up in that struggle. They left Tekirdagh and went to the town of "Tedarvaj Karaghaj" which was in Greece. This is what it was called at the time but was later renamed by the Greeks to its modern name of "Alexandropolis". After reaching there, they went by train and got off at a station called "Buk" which was just outside Alexandropolis. On the train with them was a man Hovhannes would refer to as their "Bursa General". He was an Armenian that had left the army and was with them escaping. Given his experience, he was knowledgeable in the local politics and could determine their best chances of survival. In Bursa, and in Istanbul, the Armenians had influential people that could limit the harm the authorities could inflict on the local Armenians. This man was one such person and so the Armenians looked to him for leadership.

As they got off, their Bursa General advised them not to go further inland as there was a lot of poverty there. Instead, he advised they go to one of the nearby villages populated by Turks. He said: "The Turks will look after you until we figure out what to do."

My father's family did not like the idea and immediately rejected the advice. Later, however, they realised the Bursa General was right. They realised they were in a strange land and did not know anyone. They were in no position to know what course of action to take and were better off seeking help. They went back to the Bursa General and asked him to help them with his original suggestion. He agreed and arranged for them to be sent to the nearby Turkish village of Buk. My father's family was not the only family in this situation. Many other Armenian families were facing the same decisions. The Bursa General sent several families to one Turkish village and several to another.

Hovhannes found a job in Buk, just outside Alexandropol. He worked a year or so as a labourer on a railway line until 1922. After that, he and the family moved to Thessaloniki, following his brother to a place called Kalamaria. There, they stayed in a wooden hut that originally housed soldiers during the 1912 Balkan War, where the Greeks took Thessaloniki from the Ottomans. While there, Hovhannes and the other young men in the family found work as labourers in a construction site. Hovhannes remembers earning 15 Drachma per day. His brother, Krikor, did the same work but was only on 13 Drachma per day. Krikor complained to Hovhannes about the discrepancy: "That's not fair! Why do you get paid more, I do the same work as you!"

Hovhannes replied: "Why are you complaining to me? What does it have to do with me? Tell the boss."

They stayed there in Kalamaria Thessaloniki for another year or so until 1923 when they eventually left for Cyprus.

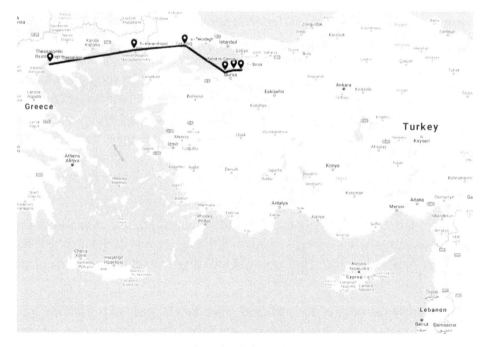

Escaping Soloz 1921

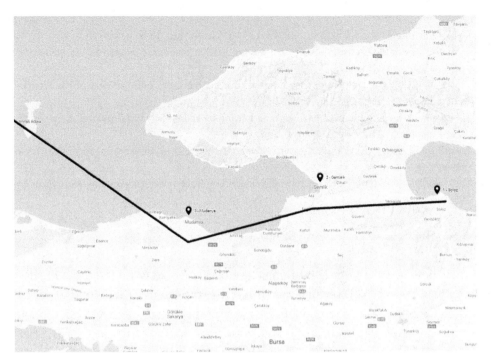

1 Soloz → 2 Gemleik → 3 Mudanya

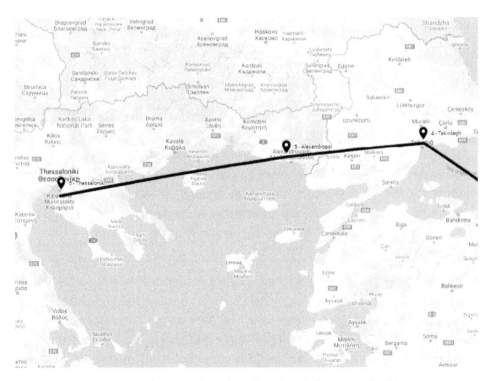

Mudanya → 4 Tekirdagh → 5 Alexadropol → 6 Thessaloniki

1. Soloz. Hovhannes and family escaped Soloz in 1921 as Ataturk advanced westward.
2. Gemleik. The family reached Gemleik but were unable to escape by ship as the advancing armies caught up with them.
3. Mudanya. With great difficulty they made it to Mudanya and, with the help of the French, caught a boat to get out.
4. Tekirdagh. After a few weeks here earning a living by selling fish and firewood, they had to escape again as Ataturk was still advancing.
5. Alexadropol. After escaping yet again, Hovhannes worked in Alexadropol for a year on a railway line.
6. Thessaloniki. The family moved onto Thessaloniki before eventually leaving for Cyprus in 1923.

Reaching Cyprus

During their time in Kalamaria Thessaloniki, the family would write letters to Chrissy who was still in Cyprus. Chrissy had not suffered at the hands of the Turks as much as the rest of the family as she had left for Cyprus a few years earlier. Even though she did not suffer like her family, Chrissy must have had it tough in Cyprus. Her husband worked as a builder and died a few years after their marriage. She could not speak Greek and so would not have been welcomed in Cyprus. Chrissy was working hard to get papers so the family could move to Cyprus. She succeeded by getting the Armenian Primate, Sarajan, of the Church in Cyprus to act as a guarantor for the family. He appointed my grandfather as a choirmaster and teacher for the church. In this way, my father's family had the right to migrate to Cyprus. They left Kalamaria for Cyprus in 1923.

To get to Cyprus, they experienced a lot of difficulty. They travelled via Egypt where they stayed for one week before eventually setting foot on the island of Cyprus. They then went to Mia Millia village and spent a week there. After that, they moved to Nicosia where the Armenian Church placed the whole family in a room next to the church. They were now among the Armenian community. My grandfather worked as a choirmaster for a few months until they brought in Mr Bedelian, a young choirmaster from Paris. They made my grandfather redundant at that point and this meant financial difficulty for the family as they were relying on his income.

Hovhannes managed to find a job selling water. He would transport water around the neighbourhood with a donkey driven cart. The water cost one Kurush (Cyprus Penny) for a few litres. He did this for a whole summer until he found a better job as a tanner. His sister, Chrissy, was working at the Agricultural Department as a Silk Manager at the time and managed to get him a job there. He worked under a Russian tanner who had escaped from the Communist Bolshevik movement in Russia and was referred to as the "White Russian". "White" being a reference to the anti-

Communist movement he was a part of. One day, while working there, the White Russian supervisor said to Hovhannes: "It's time to go for your lunch break."

Hovhannes replied: "What's the point?" By this time, Hovhannes had picked up the Greek language from the neighbourhood. The White Russian then asked: "What do you mean?"

Hovhannes responded: "What am I going to do? There is no food. You know my income is tiny. There is no food at home. We cannot afford food as there are many of us to feed at home." On that, the White Russian's heart was touched. He went to the manager of the department and discussed Hovhannes's situation with him. The manager was called Mr Noble. As my father says, he was Noble by name and noble by nature. He was a good man. He came to Hovhannes and in his broken Greek discussed the situation with him. Noble then doubled Hovhannes's pay, which meant he was now on good money. He continued to work there for several years at the Agricultural Department. They made leather gloves and leather products. Then the global financial crisis of 1931 hit Cyprus and it affected the family significantly. Hovhannes was made redundant and the financial difficulties of the family started once again.

He looked for work everywhere but no one was hiring. He found the odd temporary job painting and decorating a house and took whatever he could find but it was not enough. He had a family of his own at this time to support. He had married Nouritsa in 1927 and had his first child Margaret in 1928 and then Arshalouys in 1931. The 1931 crisis that hit Cyprus really created a lot of problems for Hovhannes. He eventually found a job in the village of Mavrovouni, working at the mine there. His brother Zareh also found a job there. They went together, leaving behind their families in Nicosia. They rented a house in Lefka where they stayed while away from the family. The polluted air in the mines made Hovhannes very sick and he could not work for weeks. During this time, he sent for his family to come to Lefka so they could look after him as he was in such a bad way. He did not want his family to come but was forced to bring them as he needed help. He continued to work while ill for a time but then had to stop completely. Then his two daughters Margaret and Arshalouys also got ill. This is when he realised they could not live like this so decided to return to Nicosia. He was in Mavrovouni for 2 months but got paid only for half that time as his illness prevented him from working. He got paid 5 Cyprus Pounds for the time he did work. At that time that was good money.

On his return to Nicosia, Baron Sultanian offered him a job working with battery acid. It was not a great job. When handling the acid, it often would splash onto him and burn holes in his clothes. It did not pay much either, only get a shilling per day. This was not enough to pay for the rent and provide for a whole family. He did not drink or smoke so did not have the expenses many others had. But then his clothes were being damaged and replacing them cost money. He was forced to leave in search for higher pay. Baron Sultanian told him about a distributor job going at the local paper. At the time, the paper published "Broini English" and he started working there. It did not pay more but at least his clothes were not being damaged. After working for several months there, things came to a head. He did not get along with the owner's wife, an Armenian from Istanbul. She would cause Hovhannes a lot of headache. One day Hovhannes's boss could see that he was in a lot of stress and told Hovhannes to take a day off to relax and calm down. This triggered something in Hovhannes and he just quit his job there and then in the heat of the moment.

Later when he had a chance to think about things more clearly, he realised he could no longer put any food on the table. His one shilling per day was no more. He did not know what to do. He used to work as a Tanner before this but there was no Tanner work at this time. His mother, Flora, told him to go for a walk to calm down. However, the stress would follow Hovhannes wherever he went. There was no food in the house and Hovhannes felt alone in his troubles. It seemed to him that no one cared. His sister, Chrissy, was looking out for him though. She would earn money by renting out part of her house. She asked if Hovhannes wanted to offer up part of his house for rent. Then something better came along. After Hovhannes left the paper, they hired a man called Puzant to replace him. It turned out they were not happy with him. They were not happy with the way he would distribute the papers so they sacked him. Hovhannes's sister heard about this and contacted the owner to see if they would take Hovhannes back. They did, and even raised his pay to a shilling and a half per day. Hovhannes worked there until 1940 around the time of the Second World War. When the war started, the British took the paper from the owner, Puzant, to help them control the war propaganda. Hovhannes continued working under the British ownership for another 5 years. In 1945 when the war ended, a Cypriot called Jacovides bought the paper. He was not a good businessman and lead the Paper into financial difficulties. It reached a point where he could not afford to pay Hovhannes's wages. Hovhannes was owed money and would go to Mr Jacovides pleading with him to get paid. He was not asking for a loan, just to get paid for the work he had done. Mr Jacovides would put him off: "I will give it tomorrow. I can't pay now but will."

Mr Jacovides's brother, Janko, came over from Africa to help turn the business around. He succeeded and for Hovhannes that meant his wages went up, eventually to 14 Cyprus Pounds per week. The money was good and he continued to work there until 1971. In parallel to working at the paper, Hovhannes started a Tannery business from home. He started the business when the war started, as there was big demand for leather goods then. This business was very successful and he made a lot of money. He used this money to build his house where the whole family could live in comfort after many years of struggle. This house was the lovely house I was born into in 1939 when my father's life improved.

Summary Thoughts

At the end of the interview, Hovhannes summarised his thoughts on the Armenian Genocide that he personally experienced with these words. "I cannot say all the Turkish people are bad people. The people of Turkey are very good people. However, the leaders of the time made them do bad things. Moreover, those bad things were done by the murderers that the leaders let out from the prisons. Those criminals performed the Genocide and the forced marches. The Turks say there was no Genocide. The Turkish people are good people but the Government at the time: Talat Pasha, Enver Pasha and Jemal Pasha were the people that committed the Genocide. In a speech, Hitler said the Armenians were victims of Genocide and no one remembered it. Therefore, Hitler said, they could do the same to the Jews. Is it possible the Turks pretend to not know these truths? From what I know of Turks they are good people and they shouldn't say these things. Maybe admitting so will mean heavy compensation and that's what they cannot accept it. We were very happy with the Turks but with these things we were not so happy. The ordinary Turks did not do these things. The Turkish government made these things happen. It was like so."

Epilogue

My mother was only about 4 years old when her brother, Mesrob, was murdered while out tending sheep in the fields. This horror was quickly followed by the murder of her father Garabed and of her brother Alexan. The Turkish authorities rounded them up, along with all the men of the village, and murdered them. Many of the women of her village that remained married Turkish men in order to save their own lives. By doing so, they effectively renounced their Armenian heritage and accepted a new Turkish heritage. My mother's older sister, Nazely, was one such woman and reluctantly married an unpleasant man called Ahmed. He forced Nazely's new-born child to die as she was born a girl and not a boy. The women that did not marry, and so did not accept a Turkish heritage, were murdered. My grandmother, Elsa, was one such woman. In a traumatised state, she hid her youngest children Melkon and my mother Nouritsa before going to the Turkish thugs to be killed at their hands. Her last words were a request for her other daughter Nazely to do what she could to save her younger siblings. Nazely managed to do that. She took Melkon to live with her and her Turkish husband and handed my mother over to a Turkish couple in another village. My mother was looked after very well by the Turkish couple for a number of years. They really did love her and were raising her as best they could in the Turkish tradition they knew. This did not last, however, as the Armenian community set about trying to rebuild their world devastated by the Ottoman Turks. This happened after the Ottomans were defeated in the First World War. My mother was taken to her father's brother in Gessaria but he was not able to look after her. He left her at the Armenian orphanage there. The orphanage did the best they could for her under difficult circumstances. They tried to reunite her with her oldest brother Mihran, who had survived the war and was now in Adana, by sending her there in a horse drawn cart. During this 6-day trip, my mother nearly died as she was forced to walk part of the way in the snow and cold. Physically exhausted, she collapsed in the snow and was moments from death. Fortunately, a family came to her rescue, spotting her in the snow they saved her and took her to Adana. In Adana, she was not reunited with her brother but instead went to school and was taught Armenian for the first time. Then came the rise of Mustafa Kemal Ataturk and the orphanage had to close and move the children so they were not massacred. She was taken to Cyprus and left with an Armenian family to be their in-house help. She eventually met my father, Hovhannes, and got married. Though things improved for her at this point, there were still many hard times to follow.

My father's traumatic childhood started when he was about 11 years old. During the First World War, he was forced to leave his village along with his family and walk for days to various remote villages. This was during a time where there was information coming through unofficial channels of the genocide being perpetrated against the

Armenian minority community in Ottoman Turkey. In this period, Hovhannes lived in fear from the persecution that Armenians faced and experienced numerous attempts on their lives. This included a crazed man chasing after him with a sword for simply being Armenian. Having spent three years away from home, my father's family eventually returned and rebuilt their lives. The Greco-Turkish war of 1919, however, resulted in Ataturk overrunning my father's village and the need for him to flee. With hundreds of thousands of fellow refugees, my father's family escaped to Greece and then to Cyprus where they started from scratch. They worked their way out of poverty and suffered a lot, including the death of their first-born Margaret from malnutrition. I was named after her.

My parents suffered at the time of the genocide but also were left psychologically scarred. My father would have nightmares until the end of his life and my mother would regularly have to console him. My mother was toughened up by her experiences. Many would feel uncomfortable if they had to kill an animal but not my mother. We kept chickens in our garden and she would cut off the head of a live chicken with no hesitation. My father, however, was the more optimistic of the two. He would always see the best in people. With a background like that, you can see how my mother would have a lot of psychological problems. You can also forgive her for telling the stories of her childhood to me, her eight-year-old daughter. The inevitable consequence, however, is the daughter will develop an inherent fear herself. That is what happened to me. My mother's past influenced my life significantly. I was brought up with my mother's stories, which made me very nervous about living among the Turks in Cyprus. British rule, however, meant I could feel safe. This started to change as EOKA triggered a coup in Cyprus followed by a Turkish invasion. My fears really caught fire at that point. I was caught up in war and knew I had to leave my homeland at the first opportunity.

When the opportunity came, I left for London. It was a hard journey through Europe by train to Paris, where we stayed for a few weeks before leaving for London. Being forcibly separated from Robert on that journey made a bad situation even worse. The difficulties we faced in London when we eventually got there did not help me recover from my traumatic experiences. There were, however, glimmers of hope. God sent me the help I needed exactly when I needed it. The French boys on the train and Mikis were truly heaven sent. My boss and friendly neighbours in London and family were also a massive blessing. How could I have got through everything without them?

Many years later when my grandson was born, he brought great joy to our lives. Baret and Katerina named him John, the English form of my father's name Hovhannes. As his parents both worked when he was born, Robert and I were honoured with the task of looking after him and what a pleasure that was. I was reminded of how my son Baret was looked after by my parents, as Robert and I had to work when he was born. I remembered how I wished I could spend more time with Baret and how wonderful the short periods I could spend with him were. This experience made me think about how important it is for Baret to have as much quality time with John as possible. As such, I would ensure that John would have his afternoon nap and be rested and calm for when Baret could come over. John's excitement at seeing his father filled me with joy. John was always such a happy child, laughing all the time. He would play with us when we tried to dress him after a bath. Robert would have to catch him and hold him while I quickly put his clothes on. To put him to sleep, I figured out that Dean Martin songs worked best. As he got older, he would thoughtfully play Dean Martin songs for us on his CD player, knowing how we liked his music. Robert and I tasted a wonderful second slice of parenthood looking after John. We experienced the joys of seeing him walk for the first time and his excitement on a magical trip to Euro Disney. We also experienced many anxieties when he got sick or when we temporarily lost him in a crowd. These anxieties, however, are the normal ones that most people face in their lives. Thank God he lives at a time and place where the political situation is relatively stable. One of my hopes in writing this is for Baret, Katerina and John to have a record of their history and appreciate the relative stability of the world they live in.

My guilt for leaving my parents, however, has always been with me. Seeing my mother's tearful face at the end of each subsequent visit before their passing was hard. I tried but did not succeed to bring them to live with us in London. She wanted me to tell the world about what happened to her. She was angry about all the things she had to endure and wanted people to know about them. She said she would forgive me for leaving her if I did and I promised her that I would. I developed cancer a few years back and fortunately survived it following a successful operation. During this time, however, the promise I had made to my mother was at the front of my mind. I tried many times to write her story to fulfil that promise but found it a struggle. Then, out of the blue, my nephew Haig said to me that I should write my mother's story. We were talking about the family history and he said he would help me do it. Hearing this was such a weight off my shoulders. We spent many hours talking about the past as he set to work extracting the information he felt was needed. This work documenting my mother's story is the result of that effort and is now available to anyone with an interest to read it. My mother went through so much seeing her family murdered and having to grow up without them. At least I can now say I have kept my promise to my mother.

Printed in Great Britain
by Amazon